FINANCIAL MANAGEMENT FOR THE SMALL BUSINESS

A Practical Guide

FOURTH EDITION

Colin Barrow

Published in
association with
The Royal Bank
of Scotland

KOGAN
PAGE

First published in 1984
Second edition 1988
Third edition 1995
Reprinted 1997
Fourth edition 1998

Kogan Page Limited
120 Pentonville Road
London N1 9JN

© Colin Barrow 1984, 1988, 1995, 1998

British Library Cataloguing in Publication Data

A CIP record for this book is available from the British Library.

ISBN 0 7494 2645 4

Printed and bound in Great Britain by Clays Ltd, St Ives plc

Contents

Big response
to small business needs

What makes the Royal Bank of Scotland stand out when it comes to setting up your own business?

. . . .

When you're setting up your own business, choosing a bank is one of many major decisions you have to make and it's important to get it right. In an ideal world, your bank manager will understand both your immediate needs as well as your long-term objectives, support you as your business grows and help you to make the right decisions at critical times.

Following extensive research among its customers, The Royal Bank of Scotland has developed a unique, tailored service reflecting these principles for people who are just starting out or already run a small business. 'We asked a wide range of businesses what they wanted from a bank, evaluated their comments and then we used them to redefine our service,' says Ian Henderson, head of business marketing with the Royal Bank.

Twice-nominated Small Business Bank of the Year, the Royal Bank remains a clear leader in customer service. Other accolades include being chosen as one of the two top banks in the UK for franchise finance and, in two independent surveys of banks and building societies, it was the only high street bank in the top category for customer service.

RELATIONSHIP

So what makes the Royal Bank stand out? One unique feature is its team of dedicated business relationship managers who have sole responsibility for start-ups and smaller owner-managed business customers.

'One complaint against banks in the past was lack of continuity – customers got to know their manager only to find that after a short time he or she had to move on,' says Ian Henderson. 'Business relationship managers are in place for a minimum of four years to provide the continuity that customers want and have the time to give them their undivided attention. Their performance is measured according to the quality of service offered to customers.'

Business relationship managers are locally based but freed from the supervisory and administrative role of a branch manager. As a result, they focus solely on customer needs and often spend more time on their customers' premises than behind their own desks. 'The aim is to get an understanding of each business and its potential, something that is particularly relevant to people setting up their own business,' says Ian Henderson.

Every small business has its own special needs but the Royal Bank also recognises that certain specialist areas may need extra support. For example, it has appointed a number of healthcare relationship managers who are dedicated to helping doctors, dentists, vets, retail chemists and others in the health business. 'This exclusive focus gives our business relationship managers a good insight into the issues and problems behind starting up a business,' says Ian Henderson. 'They are trained to understand the small business sector and bring together a whole range of specialist financial services. This means they are in a position to deliver an outstanding service to their customers by identifying and addressing their real financial needs.'

Once a business relationship manager knows a business, it is very much part of his or her job to play a pro-active role in looking after the customer. This may involve helping to maximise the return on surplus business funds or pointing out the most appropriate and cost-effective way of raising finance. In addition, they are equipped to provide rapid responses to customers' financial requirements with lending decisions guaranteed within 48 hours.

INNOVATIVE

The Royal Bank is always on the look-out for new and innovative services to meet the needs of today's ever-changing business environment. Royline, the bank's sophisticated electronic banking system, has been upgraded to keep pace with the latest technological developments, with a Windows version now available.

In addition, we have developed a business plan software package which takes the hassle out of writing a business plan. The package will ask you a series of questions about yourself, your idea and your business intentions. All you have to do is type in the answers and the package will produce a draft business plan.

For new businesses, this start-up pack is available either from local branches or by calling freephone 0800 521607.

'Every big business was once a small business. They are the wealth creators of tomorrow and we want to help as many as possible to turn into bigger businesses by providing them with all the banking services they need to achieve that goal,' says Ian Henderson. 'Over the year, the Royal Bank has helped thousands of companies do just that, underlining its recognition of the importance of start-up and owner-managed businesses to the well-being of the economy. We now operate what we believe to be the most far-reaching customer service programme in British banking. Based on our conviction that quality of services is the key to fostering strong and enduring relationships with all our customers. 'The result so far, both from start-up businesses and those that have been in existence for some time, is that this approach is what our customers want and, even more important for them, it really works.'

Preface to the Fourth Edition

When the first edition of this book was written in 1983, the small business sector of the UK economy had changed little since the 1950s. The self-employment population had oscillated in a band between 1.8 and 2 million throughout the whole period. For reasons which have now become part of history, the climate for enterprise in this country has changed profoundly in recent years. The number of self-employed has risen to over 3.7 million, and now nearly one person in every eight works for themselves. This has not been a phenomenon unique to the UK. The self-employed in the USA had been a declining population since 1928. Since then their number has risen from 7.5 million to over 11 million. Across the world the spirit of enterprise has been gaining momentum. Small businesses are being created in greater number everywhere, including China and other bastions of communism such as Russia and Eastern Europe. In Western Europe, 19 million people work for themselves. Every other measure of entrepreneurial activity shows a steeply rising curve. Venture capital organisations have risen from 20 in 1979 to 180 in 1998, and the amount they have invested in new ventures has risen correspondingly from £150 million to more than £2 billion.

Managers in larger organisations have also been swept along in the tide of entrepreneurial enthusiasm. Management buy-outs, a virtually unheard of phenomenon in 1978, consumed the lion's share of venture capital by 1998. Bank lending to small firms and such other forms of financing as leasing, hire purchase and trade credit are at substantial and rising levels.

Alongside this sharp rise in new 'entrepreneurs' has come an urgent requirement to become financially literate, an essential prerequisite to raising finance and using it wisely. Further pressure for awareness of matters financial has been applied by the Insolvency Act and wrongful trading legislation, making it an offence for directors to continue trading once they know – or should have known – their business is in trouble.

This book is intended to help those who find business finance confusing. A heavy fog seems to descend as soon as anyone approaches this field for the first time. Whether running or setting up a business, getting a first taste of responsibility for accounts or taking a business course, the first steps towards an understanding of finance are the most difficult. The consequences of failing to understand business finance are not the same for everyone. The student simply fails an exam, while the businessman all too often loses his business, and the executive gets fired. Competition is generally greater today and the margin for mistakes smaller.

Alongside this rapid growth in entrepreneurship, has come the inevitable tide of business closures. Over 400,000 small firms closed their doors in 1997/8. Recessions are a good test of an entrepreneur's financial skills. In the recession of the early 1990s, over 600,000 small firms were closing each year. Across Europe over 210,000 limited companies floundered each year.

The single most common cause is poor financial control. Indeed, surveys of business failure routinely indicate a third of failures are accounted for in this manner. People running small businesses frequently leave financial questions to their accountants to sort out at the year end. They often have the mistaken belief that keeping the books is an activity quite divorced from the 'real' task of getting customers or making products.

By the time the first set of figures is prepared most small businesses are already too far down the road to financial failure to be saved. The final accounts become all too final and a good business proposition has been ruined by financial illiteracy. The few businessmen who do ask the way, perhaps of an accountant or bank manager, often do not understand the terms being used to explain the situation.

The book begins with an introduction to the key financial statements. All too often these vital building blocks are missed out by those trying to come to grips with the problem of poor profits and a negative cash flow.

With this foundation, the tools of financial analysis are explained in Part 2, and these are the key to controlling a business successfully. If you can imagine trying to drive a car without any instruments at all, you will have some impression how unsatisfactory it would be to run a business without financial controls.

Part 3 covers the field of business planning and budgeting. Most new ventures cannot get off the ground without a sound business plan and existing businesses cannot grow without one.

A chapter is devoted to the important task of writing up and presenting a business plan. As this is the 'ticket of entry' to capital, it is as important for the business plan to look right as it is for the business proposal itself to be soundly based.

The whole book has been revised and updated to bring it right up to date.

Much of the material in this book has been used with business and academic audiences in the UK and mainland Europe over recent years. I should like to record my appreciation of those 'students' who helped me to focus on these key financial issues and to sharpen up my thinking generally. In particular, I am grateful to the participants of the Graduate Enterprise Programme at Stirling University, Cranfield University of Management and on the Entrepreneurship Programme at Suffolk University in Boston, Massachusetts, USA; those on the Small Business Programmes at the University of Greenwich; and people attending the Royal Borough of Kensington and Chelsea's new business courses. I am also grateful to directors, executives and managers of the following companies whose financial training programmes have included much of this material: Abbott Laboratories, Ash and Lacy, Englehard Industries, ICL, Johnson & Johnson, Leyland Paints, Seddon Atkinson, Seagram Distillers, Tandem Computers, Forte, Schwarzkopf, Ruberoid, the Managers Group of Companies, Manders Paints and Wyeth Laboratories.

Colin Barrow
April 1998

Part 1: Understanding Key Financial Statements

Chapter 1
The Balance Sheet –
Where we are now

There is a much told Irish story of the driver lost on his travels between Dublin and Cork. He stopped to ask the way of a passing farmer, who replied, 'If I were going to Cork I wouldn't start from here.'

For people in business this is an all too pertinent answer. We nearly always need a good idea of where we are now if we are to have any chance of reaching our goal. But either through pressures of more immediate tasks, or the nagging feeling that we will not like the answers, sizing up the financial situation is a job relegated to the bottom of the pile.

Even in our private lives it is helpful to 'strike a balance' when important financial issues are at stake. Questions such as should we move house, buy a boat, a new car, or take a holiday, involve us in an informal sizing up of the situation before making a decision.

A personal experience

This example looks at the finances of Terry Brown. She has become a little confused by the complexity of her financial affairs and has decided to get things sorted out. In short, she wants to know where she is.

If you were to summarise your present financial position it would contain, at least, some elements of the following example:

Terry Brown – Financial position today (28 March) 1

	£
Cash	50
House	50,000
Mortgage	45,000
Money owed by sister (Jackie)	135
Overdraft	100
Car (Citroen 2CV)	1,000
Credit cards	50
Jewellery and paintings	350
Hire purchase (on various goods)	500
Furniture	500

This information tells us something of Terry's circumstances, but until we organise the information we cannot really understand her true financial position.

Terry believes that in money matters things divide neatly into two: things you have and things you owe, with the latter usually exceeding the former. So, using this concept and slightly different words, we could show the same information in the following manner. On the right-hand side we have made a list of Terry's *Assets*: what she has done with the money she has had. On the left is listed where she got the money from to pay for these assets: the *Liabilities and Claims* against her.

Terry Brown – Financial position today (28 March) 2

Liabilities and Claims (Where I got the money from)	£	Assets (What I have done with the money)	£
Overdraft	100	Cash	50
Mortgage	45,000	House	50,000
Hire purchase	500	Car	1,000
Credit cards	50	Jewellery and paintings	350
Total claims by other people	45,650	Money owed by sister	135
My Capital	6,385	Furniture	500
Total of my and other people's money	52,035	My Assets	52,035

You may have got a little lost towards the bottom of the left-hand column. This is simply because we have to try and show the complete picture of Terry's financial affairs. She has acquired £52,035 worth of assets and must have provided an identical sum from

4

one source or another. We can find only £45,650 owed to other people. The only reasonable assumption is that Terry herself must have put in the balance over the past years. In other words, she has put her past salary or wages towards buying the assets.

Now while Terry might be happy with the help we have given her so far, it is unlikely she will be completely satisfied. Like the rest of us, she probably considers events as long- or short-term in nature. Even though we have shown a fairly dazzling picture of £50,000 + of assets, she knows she is short of cash for day-to-day living. So once again we could restructure the information on her financial position to give a clearer picture.

Terry Brown – Financial position today (28 March) 3

Liabilities (long term) (Where I got the money from)	£	Fixed Assets (long term) (What I have done with the money)	£
Mortgage	45,000	House	50,000
Hire purchase	500	Car	1,000
		Furniture	500
My Capital	6,385	Jewellery and paintings	350
	51,885		51,850
Current Liabilities (short term)		Current Assets (short term)	
Overdraft	100	Money owed by sister	135
Credit cards	50	Cash	50
	150		185
Total Liabilities	52,035	Total Assets	52,035

For example, we can now see that her short-term financial position is dominated by the money her sister owes her. If that is safe, then all current liabilities can be met. If it is not safe, and that money is unlikely to be repaid quickly, the position is not so good. There is an accounting convention according to which 'current' liabilities are those that we will have to pay within a year. Similarly, 'current' assets will turn into cash within a year.

We are getting very close to having a *Balance Sheet* of Terry's financial position. One further adjustment will reveal all. It is vital that both the long- and short-term financial positions are readily visible to the examiner. Terry's day-to-day assets and liabilities need to be clearly highlighted. What we are looking for is the net position: how much she currently owes, subtracted from how much she has.

By redrafting the financial position, we shall see the whole picture more clearly. £51,850 is tied up in *fixed assets* and £35 is tied up in *net current assets*. All these have been *financed by* £6,385 of Terry's capital and £45,500 has been provided by a mortgage and a hire purchase company.

The public picture

Terry Brown found it useful to have a clear picture of her current financial position. A business will find such a picture essential. While most people are responsible only to themselves and their families, businesses have a wider audience. Partners, bankers, shareholders, financial institutions, Customs and Excise and the Inland Revenue are only a few of the possible interested parties, apart from the owners' and managers' interest in the financial situation which is taken for granted.

Terry Brown – Balance Sheet at 28 March

		£
Fixed Assets		
House		50,000
Car		1,000
Furniture		500
Jewellery and paintings		350
		51,850
Current Assets		
Money owed by sister		135
Cash		50
		185
Less Current Liabilities		
Overdraft		100
Credit cards		50
		150
So, Net Current Assets		35
Total Assets, *less* Current Liabilities		51,885
Financed by		
My Capital		6,385
Mortgage	45,000	
Hire purchase	500	45,500
Total		51,885

All these interested parties keep track of a business's financial performance by having a series of reports, or statements, prepared. In effect a business acts as a steward of other people's money and it is to give account of this stewardship that these financial records are prepared. While these 'figure' statements provide usual evidence, it is as well to remember that the evidence is only partial: nothing in Terry's Balance Sheet has told us that she is shapely, 27 years old and currently sporting a carrot-red head of hair.

Another important limitation on these financial statements is the reliability of the figures themselves. The cash in hand figure is probably dead right, but can the same be said of the furniture values? Accountants have their own rules on how these figures are to be arrived at, but they do not pretend to anything better than an approximation. Every measuring device has inherent inaccuracies, and financial controls are no exception.

Not all the information that we need to prepare a financial statement is always readily on hand. For example, Terry has not had a statement on her credit card account since February (the preceding month), so despite the incomplete data, she has made an educated guess at the current position.

With these questions of reliability in mind, let us now look at how a business monitors and controls its financial position.

The structure of the business Balance Sheet

You might have noticed that we stopped calling Terry's statement a financial position, and called it a Balance Sheet in the last example. This is one of the principal business control reports. It is designed to show what assets the business is using at a particular time, and where it got the money to finance those assets. The Balance Sheet is usually a statement of the present position, but of course, once a business has been in existence for some time there will be historical balance sheets. These can be used to compare performance in one year (period) with another. This use of the Balance Sheet will be examined in the chapters on financial control.

It is also possible to prepare a projected Balance Sheet to show what the future financial picture might look like, given certain assumptions. We shall look at this aspect in more detail in the chapters on planning and budgeting.

You will notice a number of differences between the business Balance Sheet below and the personal one we looked at before. But there are also many basic similarities.

First, you will notice the date at the top. This is essential, as the Balance Sheet is a picture of the business at a particular moment in time. The picture could look quite different tomorrow if, for example, some of the £400 cash was spent on further fixtures and fittings. There are three columns of £s simply to make the arithmetic of the subtotals easier to calculate and understand.

You can also see that some different terms are used for the account categories. Before looking at the main elements of this Balance Sheet it will be useful to describe the key terms, assets and liabilities.

A Balance Sheet for a small business might look something like this:

Balance Sheet at 31 December, year ————

Net Assets employed	£	£	£
Fixed Assets			
Equipment/machinery		9,000	
Fixtures and fittings		3,800	12,800
Current Assets			
Stock	700		
Debtors	700		
Cash	400	1,800	
Less Current Liabilities			
Creditors		900	
Net Current Assets			
(Working Capital)			900
			13,700
Financed by			
Owner's Capital introduced	6,500		
Add net profit for year	5,000		
	11,500		
Less drawings	4,500		7,000
10-year loan from bank			6,700
			13,700

Assets

Accountants describe assets as 'valuable resources, owned by a business, which were accrued at a measurable money cost'. You can see that there are three key points in the definition:

1. To be valuable the resource must be cash, or of some use in generating current or future profits. For example, a debtor (someone who owes a business money for goods or services provided) usually pays up. When he does, the debtor becomes cash and so meets this test. If there is no hope of getting payment then you can hardly view the sum as an asset.
2. Ownership, in its legal sense, can be seen as different from possession or control. The accounting use of the word is similar but not identical. In a business, possession and control are not enough to make a resource an asset. For example, a leased machine may be possessed and controlled by a business but be owned by the leasing company. So not only is it not an asset, it is a regular expense. (More about expenses in the next chapter.)
3. Most business resources are bought for a 'measurable money cost'. Often this test is all too painfully obvious. If you pay cash for something, or promise to pay at a later date, it is clearly an asset. If the resource was manufactured by the business then money was paid in wages, materials etc during that process. There may be problems in deciding exactly what money figure to put down, but there is no problem in seeing that money has been spent.

The asset 'goodwill' is one important grey area of particular interest to those buying or selling a small business. This term is defined in the glossary.

Ranking of Assets

There is a useful convention that recommends listing assets in the Balance Sheet in their order of permanence, that is, starting out with the most difficult to turn into cash and working down to cash itself. This structure is very practical when you are looking at someone else's Balance Sheet, or comparing Balance Sheets. It can also help you to recognise obvious information gaps quickly.

Liabilities

These are the claims by people outside the business. In our examples only creditors are shown, but they could include such items as: tax; accruals; deferred income; overdrafts etc. These are also described either in the glossary or elsewhere in an appropriate place. The 'financed by' section of our example balance sheet is also considered in part as liabilities.

Current

This is the term used with both assets and liabilities to show that they will be converted into cash, or have a short life (under one year).

Now let's go through the main elements of the Balance Sheet.

Net assets employed

This is the 'What have we done with the money?' section. A business can only do three things with funds:

1. It can buy *fixed assets*, such as premises, machinery and motor cars. These are assets that the business intends to keep over the longer term. They will be used to help make profits, but will not physically vanish in the short term (unless sold and replaced, like motor cars, for example).

2. Money can be tied up in *working capital*, that is, 'things' immediately involved in the business's products (or services) that will vanish in the short term. Stocks get sold and are replaced; debtors pay up, and creditors are paid; and cash circulates. Working capital is calculated by subtracting the current liabilities from the current assets. This is the net sum of money that a business has to find to finance the working capital. In the Balance Sheet this is called the *net current assets*, but on most other occasions the term working capital is used.

3. Finally a business can put money aside over the longer term, perhaps in local government bonds or as an investment in someone else's business venture. In the latter case this could be a prelude to takeover. In the former it could be a cash reserve for future capital investment. The account category is called *investments*. It is not shown in this example as it is a fairly rare phenomenon in new or small businesses, who are usually cash hungry rather than rich.

Financed by

This section of the Balance Sheet shows where the money came from. It usually has at least three subheadings, although larger companies can have many more.

1. The *owner's capital introduced* shows the money put into the business by the proprietor. If this was the Balance Sheet of a limited company it would be called *share capital*. There could

then follow a list of different types of share, for example, preference and ordinary shares.

2. The second source of funds are the *profits* ploughed back into the business to help it grow. In this example the £5,000 profit was reduced to £500 after the owner had taken his drawings – or wages – out. So £500 was *retained* and this is the term often used to describe this ploughed-back profit. Another term in common use is *Reserves*, which conjures up pictures of sums of cash stored away for a rainy day. It is important to remember that this is not necessarily so. The only cash in a business is that shown under that heading in the current assets. The reserves, like all the other funds, are used to finance a business and are tied up in the fixed assets and working capital.

3. The final source of money to finance a business is long-term *loans* from outside parties. These loans could be in the form of debentures, a mortgage, hire purchase agreements or long-term loans from a bank. The common features of all such loans are that businesses have to pay interest on the money, and eventually repay the capital whether or not the business is successful. Conversely, if the business is a spectacular success the lenders, unlike the shareholders, will not share in the extra profits.

The ground rules, concepts and conventions

Accounting is certainly not an exact science. Even the most enthusiastic member of the profession would not make that claim. As we have already seen, there is considerable scope for interpretation and educated guesswork. Obviously, if this were to go on unbridled no one inside or outside the business would place any reliance on the figures, so certain ground rules have been laid down by the profession to help get a level of consistency into accounting information.

1. *Money measurement.* In accounting, a record is kept only of the facts that can be expressed in money terms. For example, the state of the managing director's health, or the fact that your main competitor is opening up right opposite in a more attractive outlet, are important business facts. No accounting record of them is made, however, and they do not show up on the Balance Sheet, simply because no objective monetary value can be assigned to these facts.

11

Expressing business facts in money terms has the great advantage of providing a common denominator. Just imagine trying to add typewriters and motor cars, together with a 4,000 square foot workshop, and then arriving at a total. You need a common term to be able to carry out the basic arithmetical functions, and to compare one set of accounts with another.

There is one great danger with expressing things in money terms. It suggests that all the pounds are identical. This is not always so. Pounds currently shown as cash in a Balance Sheet are not exactly the same, for example, as debtors' pounds that may not be turned into cash for many months. The ways of examining this changing value of money over time are looked at in Chapter 7.

2. *Business entity*. The accounts are kept for the business itself, rather than for the owner(s), workers, or anyone else associated with the firm. If an owner puts a short-term cash injection into his business, it will appear as a loan under current liabilities in the business account. In his personal account it will appear as an asset – money someone else owes him. So depending on which point of view you take, the same sum of money can be an asset or a liability. And as in this example, the owner and the business are substantially the same person, the possibilities of confusion are considerable. This source of possible confusion must be cleared up and the business entity concept does just that.

The concept states that assets and liabilities are always defined from the business's viewpoint. Once again it is this idea of stewardship that forces us to see the business as an entity separate from *all* outside parties.

3. *Cost concept*. Assets are usually entered into the accounts at cost. For a variety of reasons, the real 'worth' of an asset will probably change over time.

The worth, or value, of an asset is a subjective estimate which no two people are likely to agree on. This is made even more complex, and artificial, because the assets themselves are usually not for sale. So in the search for objectivity, the accountants have settled for cost as the figure to record. It does mean that a Balance Sheet does not show the current worth or value of a business. That is not its intention. Nor does it mean that the 'cost' figure remains unchanged for ever. For example, a motor car costing £6,000 may end up looking like this after two years:

Year 1		Year 2	
Fixed Assets	£	Fixed Assets	£
Motor car	6,000	Motor car	6,000
Less cumulative depreciation	1,500	*Less* cumulative depreciation	3,000
Net Asset	4,500	Net Asset	3,000

The depreciation is how we show the asset being 'consumed' over its working life. It is simply a book-keeping record to allow us to allocate some of the cost of an asset to the appropriate time period. The time period will be determined by such factors as how long the working life of the asset is. The Inland Revenue does not allow depreciation as a business expense – but it does allow tax relief on the capital expenditure. The proportion of capital purchase allowed by the Inland Revenue to be offset against tax is called the 'writing down' or 'capital allowance'. It is generally 25 per cent of the declining balance; in other words, in year one you can write down £250 on a capital purchase of £1,000, and in year two £188 (25 per cent of £750), and so on. However, in 1998/9 small and medium-sized firms were allowed to write down 40 per cent (but not cars or assets for leasing). This measure was intended to stimulate capital expenditure.

Other assets, such as freehold land and buildings, will be revalued from time to time, and stock will be entered at cost, or market value, whichever is the lower, in line with the principle of conservatism (explained on page 15).

4. *Going concern*. Accounting reports always assume that a business will continue trading indefinitely into the future – unless there is good evidence to the contrary. This means that the assets of the business are looked at simply as profit generators and not as being available for sale.

Look again at the motor car example above. In year 2, the net asset figure in the accounts, prepared on a 'going concern' basis, is £3,000. If we knew that the business was to close down in a few weeks, then we would be more interested in the car's resale value than its 'book' value: the car might fetch only £2,000 which is quite a different figure.

Once a business stops trading, we cannot realistically look at the assets in the same way. They are no longer being used in the business to help generate sales and profits. The most objective figure is what they might realise in the market place.

Anyone who has been to a sale of machinery will know the difference between book and market value!

5. *Dual aspect*. To keep a complete record of any business transaction we need to know both where money came from and what has been done with it. It is not enough simply to say, for example, that someone has put £1,000 into their business. We have to see how that money has been used.

Take a look at the example below. Column 1 has in it the figures we inherited before the owner put an extra £1,000 into the business. Column 2 shows what happened to the 'financed by' section of the Balance Sheet at the moment more money was put in. But as you can see, the Balance Sheet does not balance. It is also logically clear that we must have done something with that £1,000 the moment we received it. Column 3 shows exactly how we have used the money. It is tied up in cash. It could just as easily have been used to finance more customers (debtors) or to buy more stock, or even to pay off a bill, ie, reduce creditors.

Example: Balance Sheet changes

	1		2		3	
Net Assets employed	£	£	£	£	£	£
Fixed Assets		12,800		12,800		12,800
Current Assets						
Stock	700		700		700	
Debtors	700		700		700	
Cash	400		400		1,400	
	1,800		1,800		2,800	
Less Current Liabilities						
Creditors	(900)		(900)		(900)	
Net Current Assets		900		900		1,900
		13,700		13,700		14,700
Financed by						
Owner's Capital (less drawings)		7,000		8,000		8,000
10-year loan from bank		6,700		6,700		6,700
		13,700		14,700		14,700

However, the essential relationship of Assets = Capital + Liabilities has to be maintained. That is the basis of double entry book-keeping. You can think of it as the accounting equivalent of Newton's third law, 'For every force there is an equal and opposite reaction'.

There are two other important accounting concepts, realisation and accrual, but they can be better dealt with when the next accounting report is looked at.

Accounting conventions

These concepts provide a useful set of ground rules, but they are open to a range of possible interpretations. Over time, a generally accepted approach to how the concepts are applied has been arrived at. This approach hinges on the use of three conventions: conservatism, materiality and consistency.

Conservatism

Accountants are often viewed as merchants of gloom, always prone to take a pessimistic point of view. The fact that a point of view has to be taken at all is the root of the problem. The convention of conservatism means that, given a choice, the accountant takes the figure that will result in a lower end profit. This might mean, for example, taking the higher of two possible expense figures. Few people are upset if the profit figure at the end of the day is higher than earlier estimates. The converse is never true.

Materiality

A strict interpretation of depreciation (see *cost concept*, item 3, on page 12) would lead to all sorts of trivial paperwork. For example, pencil sharpeners, staplers and paperclips, all theoretically items of fixed assets, should be depreciated over their working lives. This is obviously a useless exercise and in practice these items are written off when they are bought.

Clearly, the level of 'materiality' is not the same for all businesses. A multinational may not keep meticulous records of every item of machinery under £1,000. For a small business this may represent all the machinery it has.

Consistency

Even with the help of those concepts and conventions, there is a fair degree of latitude in how you can record and interpret financial information. You should choose the methods that give the fairest picture of how the firm is performing and stick with them. It is very difficult to keep track of events in a business that is always changing its accounting methods. This does not mean that you are stuck with one method for ever. Any change, however, is an important step.

The Balance Sheet shown earlier, though very simple, is complete enough to demonstrate the key principles involved. A much larger or more complex business may have more account categories, but the main sections of its Balance Sheet will be much the same, and you will now be able to recognise them.

Questions

These questions may help you to make sure of your understanding of the Balance Sheet.

1. Draw up your own personal Balance Sheet, using the four stages of the Terry Brown example as your guide.
2. A friend has brought round the following information about his business and asked for your help. Put together a balance sheet for him.

The situation today (Sunday 24 April)

	£
Debtors	1,400
Creditors	1,800
Factory premises	18,000
Cash in hand	800
Tax due to be paid (should have gone out last week)	700
Equipment and machinery	7,600
Money I put in at start	18,700
Long-term loan	12,000
Money I have drawn out so far	4,000
Stock	1,400

Chapter 2
The Profit and Loss Account – Where we have been

The Balance Sheet shows the financial position of a business at a particular moment in time. Over time that picture will change, just as pictures of you, first as a baby, then as a teenager and lastly as an adult, will all be different – but nevertheless true likenesses of you. The 'ageing' process that changes a business's appearance is an event called a transaction. This takes place when anything is done that can be represented in money terms. For example, if you buy in stock, sell out to a customer or take credit, these are all events that can be expressed in money.

Dealing with transactions

Let us take a very simple example. On 6 April a new business called High Finance Limited is started. The initial share capital is £10,000 and on day 1 this money is held in the company's bank. The Balance Sheet would look something like this:

Balance Sheet for High Finance Ltd at 6 April, year ———

	£
Assets employed	
Cash at Bank	10,000
Financed by	
Share Capital	10,000

Not very profound, but it does show the true picture at that date. On 7 April things begin to happen.

Balance Sheet for High Finance Ltd at 7 April, year _____

Assets employed	£	£
Current Assets		
Cash at Bank A and in hand	15,000	
Less Current Liabilities		
Overdraft (Bank B)	5,000	
Net Current Assets		10,000
Financed by		
Share Capital		10,000

High Finance borrows £5,000 on an overdraft from another bank, taking the money out immediately in cash. This event is an accounting transaction and the new Balance Sheet is shown above.

You can see that the asset, 'cash', has gone up, while the liability, 'overdraft', has also risen. Any financial event must have at least two effects on the Balance Sheet.

On 8 April, High Finance buys in stock for resale, at a cost of £2,000, paying cash.

Balance Sheet for High Finance Ltd at 8 April, year _____

Assets employed	£	£
Current Assets		
Cash at Bank and in hand	13,000	
Stock	2,000	
	15,000	
Less Current Liabilities		
Overdraft	5,000	
Net Current Assets		10,000
Financed by		
Share Capital		10,000

The working capital has been changed, not in total, but in content. Cash has been reduced to pay for stock. However, a new asset, stock, has been acquired.

On 9 April, High Finance sells for £300 cash, stock that cost it £200.

Balance Sheet for High Finance Ltd at 9 April, year _____

Assets employed	£	£
Current Assets		
Cash at Bank and in hand	13,300	
Stock	1,800	
	15,100	
Less Current Liabilities		
Overdraft	5,000	
Net Current Assets		10,100
Financed by		
Share Capital	10,000	
Retained Earnings (reserves)	100	
		10,100

In this case cash has been increased by £300, the money received from a customer. Stocks have been reduced by £200, the amount sold. Finally, a 'profit' has been made and this can be shown, at least in this example, as Retained Earnings (or reserves).

The residual effect of *all* trading transactions is an increase or decrease in the worth of the business to the owners (shareholders in this case). Income from sales tends to increase the worth of a business. Expenses incurred in generating sales tend to decrease the worth. These events are so vital to the business that they are all monitored in a separate accounting report – the Profit and Loss Account.

So to summarise: the Balance Sheet shows the financial picture of a business at a particular moment in time. The Profit and Loss Account monitors income and expenditure over a particular period of time. The time intervals can be a week, a month, an accounting period, or a year. While we are very interested in all the components of income and expense, it is the result, the net profit (or loss), that we are most interested in. This shows the increase (or decrease) in the business's worth, over the time in question.

Some more ground rules

Before looking at the structure of the Profit and Loss Account it would be helpful to look at the accounting concepts that apply to it. These are numbered 6 and 7 to follow on from the five concepts given in Chapter 1.

6. *The realisation concept.* A particularly prudent sales manager once said that an order was not an order until the customer's

cheque had cleared: he had consumed the product; had not died as a result; and finally, he had shown every indication of wanting to buy again.

Most of us know quite different salesmen who can 'anticipate' the most unlikely volume of sales. In accounting, income is usually recognised as having been earned when the goods (or services) are despatched and the invoice sent out. This has nothing to do with when an order is received, or how firm an order is, or how likely a customer is to pay up promptly.

It is also possible that some of the products despatched may be returned at some later date – perhaps for quality reasons. This means that income, and consequently profit, can be brought into the business in one period, and have to be removed later on. Obviously, if these returns can be estimated accurately, then an adjustment can be made to income at the time.

So the 'Sales Income' figure that is seen at the top of a Profit and Loss Account is the value of the goods despatched and invoiced to customers in the period in question.

7. *The accrual concept.* The Profit and Loss Account sets out to 'match' income and expenditure to the appropriate time period. It is only in this way that the profit for the period can be realistically calculated. Suppose, for example, that you are calculating one month's profits when the quarterly telephone bill comes in. The picture might look like this:

Profit and Loss Account for January, year _____

	£
Sales Income for January	4,000
Less Telephone Bill (last quarter)	800
Profit	3,200

This is clearly wrong. In the first place, three months' telephone charges have been 'matched' against one month's sales. Equally wrong is charging anything other than January's telephone bill against January's income. Unfortunately, bills such as this are rarely to hand when you want the accounts, so in practice the telephone bill is 'accrued' for. The figure (which may even be absolutely correct if you have a meter) is put in as a provision to meet this liability when it becomes due.

With these two additional concepts we can now look at a business Profit and Loss Account.

Profit and Loss Account for a manufacturing business

Hardcourt Ltd
Profit and Loss Account for the year ended 31 December

	£
Sales	100,000
Cost of Goods Sold	65,000
Gross Profit	35,000
Selling Expenses	5,000
Administrative Expenses	14,000
Total Expenses	19,000
Net Profit before Tax	16,000
Tax at 25%	4,000
Net Profit after Tax	12,000

This is a simplified P and L Account for a small manufacturing company. A glance at it will show that we have at least three sorts of profit to measure in the Profit and Loss Account. The first, *gross profit*, is the difference between the sales income that we have generated and all the costs that have gone into making the goods.

Hardcourt Ltd
Profit and Loss Account for the year ended 31 December

	£	£	£
Sales			100,000
Manufacturing Costs			
Raw materials opening stock	30,000		
Purchases in period	25,000		
	55,000		
Less Raw materials closing stock	15,500		
Cost of Materials used		39,500	
Direct Labour Cost		18,000	
Manufacturing Overhead Cost			
Indirect Labour	4,000		
Workshop Heat, Light and Power	3,500		
Total Manufacturing Costs		7,500	
Cost of Goods Sold			65,000
Gross Profit			35,000

Cost of goods sold

Now you may consider that everything you have spent in the business has gone into 'making' the product, but to calculate the cost of goods sold, only costs strictly concerned with making are considered. These will include the cost of all materials and the cost of manufacturing labour.

After blowing up the cost of goods sold section, Hardcourt's P and L Account could look like the one on page 21 (bottom).

This is not a complete list of items we would find in the cost of goods sold section of a manufacturer's P and L Account. For example, work in progress, plant depreciation etc, have been ignored to keep the example clear enough for the principle to be established.

Net profit before and after tax

The second type of profit we have to measure is net profit before tax (NPBT). This is arrived at by deducting all the other expenses from the gross profit. The final item to be deducted is tax, which leaves the last profit to be measured, net profit after tax (NPAT), or the much referred to 'bottom line'.

Clearly, we could arrive at net profit after tax by simply deducting all the expenses for the period from all the income. The reason for 'organising' the information is to help us analyse and interpret that information: in other words, to see how we made a certain profit or loss in a particular trading period.

Profit and Loss Account for a service business

All the basic principles and practices of the manufacturing business apply to a service or professional business. The main area of difference will be in the calculation of gross profit. For example, a consultancy organisation's P and L Account could look as follows:

Thames Consultants

	£	£
Sales	65,000	
Fees paid to consultants	30,000	
Profit before Expenses (Gross Profit)		35,000
Expenses etc (as for any other business)		..

or a travel agency's account might look like this:

Sunburn Travel

	£
Sales	200,000
Payments to carriers	130,000
Net Commission Income (Gross Profit)	70,000
Expenses etc (as for any other business)	..

You can see that the basic principle of calculating the gross profit, or the margin that is left after the cost of 'producing' the service has been met, is being maintained.

Sales analysis

It may be useful to show the sales revenue by each major product group, and by home and export sales, if appropriate. It would be even more useful to show the gross margin by major product.

Domestic Furniture Ltd

	£	£
Sales:		
Tables	50,000	
Chairs	20,000	
Repairs etc	10,000	
		80,000
Cost of Goods Sold		50,000
Gross Profit		30,000
Less Expenses (as for any other business)		..

The structure of a Profit and Loss Account

Once a business has been trading for a few years it will have taken on a wide range of new commitments. For example, as well as the owner's money, there may be a long-term loan to be serviced (interest and capital repayments), or parts of the workshop or offices may be sublet. Now the business Profit and Loss Account will include most of the elements in the example on page 24. Like any accounting report it should be prepared in the best form for the user. The elements of this example are explained below.

(a) Sales (and any other revenues from operations).
(b) Cost of sales (or cost of goods sold). (At the moment a product is sold and its income is 'realised', so too are its costs.) See fuller explanation of cost of goods sold on page 21.

Profit and Loss Account

		£	£
1.	Sales		140,000
2.	**Cost of Sales**		
	Opening Stock	18,000	
	Purchases	74,000	
		92,000	
	Less Closing Stock	22,000	
	Cost of Goods Sold		70,000
3.	**Gross Profit**		70,000
4.	**Operating Expenses**		
	Selling	12,500	
	Administration	12,500	
	General	30,000	
	Total Expenses		55,000
5.	**Operating (or Trading) Profit**		15,000
6.	**Non-operating Revenue**		
	Investment Interest	1,000	
	Rents	500	
	Total		1,500
			16,500
7.	**Non-operating Expenses**		
	Loan Interest Paid		3,000
8.	Profit before Income Tax		13,500
9.	Tax at 25%		3,375
10.	Profit after Tax		10,125

	£
Opening Stock	18,000
Plus Purchases	74,000
Equals Goods Available for Sale	92,000
Less Closing Stock	22,000
Cost of Goods Sold	70,000

(c) Gross profit – the difference between sales and cost of sales.
(d) Operating expenses: selling – administration and general.
(e) Operating profit: the difference between gross profit and operating expense.
(f) Non-operating revenues – other revenues including interest – rent etc.

(g) Non-operating expenses – financial costs and other expenses not directly related to the running of the business.
(h) Profit before income tax.
(i) Provision for income tax.
(j) Net income – or profit and loss.

Just to make sure you understand the process and structure of the Profit and Loss Account, work through the examples at the end of the chapter.

Accounting requirements of the Companies Acts

A very sizeable majority of small businesses are either sole traders or partnerships. Such businesses have some latitude as to how they show their accounts, but obviously they would be prudent to follow guidelines such as those in these first two chapters.

Limited companies do have to prepare accounts and file them with the Registrar of Companies. The Companies Act 1985 laid down standard Balance Sheet and Profit and Loss Account formats, and various later Companies Acts have further modified these. These are similar to those we have been looking at, but by no means as clear and understandable to the layman, as they are really designed for company auditors' use.

For example, logic would suggest that the balance sheet should look like this, with the Assets clustered at the top and the Liabilities (creditors over one year includes long-term loans, and shareholders' funds) at the bottom.

'Logical' Balance Sheet		£
Fixed Assets		230
Current Assets Stock Debtors	140	
Less Creditors	100	
Net Current Assets		40
Total Assets less Current Liabilities		270
Creditors: Amounts falling due after more than 1 year		100
Share Capital	100	
Reserves	70	
Total Shareholders' funds		170
		270

However, the Companies Act requires a balance sheet looking something like this:

Balance Sheet required by Companies Act		£
Fixed Assets		230
Current Assets Stock Debtors	140	
Less Creditors	100	
Net Current Assets		40
Total Assets less Current Liabilities		270
Less Creditors over one year		100
		170
Share Capital	100	
Reserves	70	
Total Shareholders' Funds		170

Here we show how the shareholders' funds alone have been used. The top portion of the balance sheet is a mish-mash of long-term and short-term items and of assets and liabilities. For the purpose of analysis it makes no difference which layout you use. For management accounts it makes sense to use a layout that can be readily understood by managers!

Questions

1. Record the effects of the following events on the Balance Sheet, noting the changes you would make to existing figures, or by adding new items as necessary. Remember every transaction must have at least two effects on the Balance Sheet. Look back at the dual aspect concept on page 14 to remind yourself how this works. After you have finished recording the events, prepare a closing Balance Sheet.

   1. Stock costing £250 was sold for £400, received in cash.
   2. Freehold land costing £15,000 was purchased by paying £1,500 cash and taking a 20-year mortgage for the balance.
   3. A company car costing £3,000 was purchased, High Finance agreeing to pay the garage cash in 60 days.
   4. Stock costing £3,000 was purchased, the supplier agreeing to payment within 30 days.

5. Stock costing £1,800 was sold for £2,700, the customer agreeing to pay within 120 days.
(All these transactions can be assumed to have happened over a period of a few days.)

High Finance Ltd
Balance Sheet at 10 April, year _____

	£	£
Fixed Assets		–
Working Capital		
Current Assets		
Stock	1,800	
Cash	13,300	
	15,100	
Less Current Liabilities		
Overdraft	5,000	
Net Current Assets		10,100
Total		10,100
Financed by		
Share Capital		10,000
Retained earnings (reserves)		100
		10,100

2. The following is a list of items you would normally expect to find in a Profit and Loss Account. Unfortunately they are not in the right order. Re-arrange them in the correct order, and so arrive at the business's net profit after tax.

	£
Purchases during the period	90,000
Miscellaneous Expenses	1,900
Interest Expenses	3,000
Sales	174,000
Rent from sub-letting part of workshop	400
Provision for income tax	3,275
Opening Stock	110,000
Administration Expenses	21,000
Selling Expenses	7,000
Advertising Expenses	2,100
Closing Stock at end of the period	73,700

Chapter 3
Cash Flow and Funds Flow –
Where we are going

One of the characteristics that most new or small businesses have in common is a tendency to change their size and shape quickly. In the early months and years customers are few, and each new customer (or particularly big order) can mean a large percentage increase in sales. A large increase in sales in turn means an increase in raw materials and perhaps more wages and other expenses. Generally, these expenses have to be met before your customer pays up, not, however, before his order appears on your Profit and Loss Account as additional income, and perhaps profit. Remember that income is realised in the P and L Account when the 'goods' are despatched and the invoice raised. But until the money comes in, the business has to find cash to meet its bills. If it cannot find the cash to meet these day-to-day bills then it becomes 'illiquid' and very often goes bust.

Overtrading

Bankers have a name for it. They call it overtrading. Put simply it means taking on more business than you have the cash to finance. The following simple example will illustrate the problem.

A case study in overtrading (and how to avoid doing it)

The High Note Company is a new business, set up to retail music products, including sheet music, instruments and tapes/records. Customers will include schools, colleges and other institutions who will expect trade credit, and members of the public who will pay cash. The owner plans to put in £10,000 and he has high hopes of borrowing a further £10,000 from his bank. The premises being taken on are in good repair, but £12,500 will have to be spent on fixtures and fittings. This will leave £7,500 to meet immediate trading expenses, but customers' cash should come in quickly enough to meet day-to-day bills. The rent, rates and other basic expenses (telephone, heat, light, power and transport) should come to £27,600 over the full year. (This will include running repairs and renewals of fittings.) Apart from the owner, staff wages and book-keeping costs will be £12,000. It is also planned to spend £250 per month on advertising. The first six months are going to be the most crucial; however, High Note's owner is confident of sales of £60,000 in that period, and the average mark-up across the product range will be 50 per cent. On this basis the following Profit and Loss Account was prepared:

High Note
Projected P and L Account – six months April-September*

	£	£
Sales		60,000
Cost of Goods Sold		30,000
Gross Profit		30,000
Expenses†		
Rent, Rates etc	13,800	
Wages	6,000	
Advertising	1,500	21,300
Net Profit before Interest Charges and Tax		8,700

This appears to be a very respectable profit, certainly enough to support a £10,000 loan, and perhaps enough to support the owner. However, this is not the whole picture. Customers will not pay on the nail; suppliers will want cash as this is a new business; wage earners and the landlord will want immediate payment. So the cash position will look more like the table opposite.

The top of the cash flow forecast shows the cash coming into the business each month. While High Note had a sales income in the first six months of £60,000, only £48,000 cash came in. Some customers have yet to pay up. Also the owner's start-up capital comes in, in April, along with the loan capital.

---

* Note that as this is a six-month period, only half the expenses are included.
† Strictly speaking, we should either depreciate or write off the furniture and fixtures. In this simplified case, this has been omitted.

The middle of the cash flow forecast shows the cash payments out of the business. Purchases of instruments, sheet music, books, records and tapes make up the largest element of this. £30,000's worth of purchases are needed to support sales of £60,000 (gross margin 50 per cent), and at least one month's stock has to be available in September to meet October's demand.

High Note
Six-month Cash Flow Forecast

	April £	May £	June £	July £	Aug £	Sept £	Totals for Sales and Purchases only £
Cash Receipts in*							
Sales	4,000	5,000	5,000	7,000	12,000	15,000	48,000
Owner's Capital	10,000						
Loan Capital	10,000						
Total Cash in	24,000	5,000	5,000	7,000	12,000	15,000	
Cash Payments out							
Purchases	5,500	2,950	4,220	7,416	9,332	9,690	39,108
Rent, Rates etc.	2,300	2,300	2,300	2,300	2,300	2,300	
Wages	1,000	1,000	1,000	1,000	1,000	1,000	
Advertising	250	250	250	250	250	250	
Fixtures and Fitting	12,500	–	–	–	–	–	
Total Cash out	21,550	6,500	7,770	10,966	12,882	13,240	
Cash Balances							
Monthly Cash Balance	2,450	(1,500)	(2,770)	(3,966)	(882)	1,760	
Balance brought forward	–	2,450	950	(1,820)	(5,786)	(6,668)	
Balance to carry forward or Net Cash Flow	2,450	950	(1,820)	(5,786)	(6,668)	(4,908)	

So £39,108 must be paid out to suppliers. Following this are all the other cash payments listed in the months they are to be paid.

The bottom of the cash flow forecast shows the cash balances. The monthly cash balance shows the surplus (or deficit in brackets) for each month; the balance brought forward shows the amount brought forward from the preceding month, and the balance to carry forward shows the cumulative cash position, or net cash flow as it is usually called.

For the first two months of trading, High Note has enough cash to meet its needs. But from June to August the company

---

* Value added tax is paid and collected by all businesses with a turnover greater than £49,000 per annum (1998). To keep this example simple, VAT has been ignored, but you should remember that you will probably have to show VAT separately; that is, Sales, and VAT on Sales separately, and quarterly cash payments to the Customs and Excise.

needs £6,668 cash to meet current needs. By this stage most of the owner's time is probably being spent badgering good customers to pay up early, very often driving them into the arms of competitors, pleading with suppliers for credit, or worse still, searching out inferior sources of supply. The business is now being constrained by a cash corset and the needs of the market place have become a low priority.

Forecasting cash needs

Fortunately, this cash flow statement is a projection and High Note has still time to prevent such problems. From the trend of the figures it looks as though the cash deficit will be wiped out by Christmas. If this is the case perhaps an overdraft could provide an answer. However, Christmas is probably a high sales period so the cash position might deteriorate again. As a general rule, if a business is alternating between periods of cash surplus and cash deficit, an overdraft is the answer. If there are no periods of cash surplus then the business is under-capitalised. In other words, either the owner must put in more cash or, if the profit warrants it, more outside money can be borrowed, long term.

While High Note was largely a fictional example, the experience for new and small businesses is an all too common one. It is vital to forecast cash flow month by month for the year ahead. It would be prudent to look ahead for a further year or so on a quarterly basis. The ratios explained in Chapter 6, Control of Working Capital, will provide some pointers as to how the cash flow forecast can be made. If you are asking other people to invest in your business proposition, the cash flow forecast will be even more interesting than the projected profit. This forecast will reveal your chance of survival long enough to collect your 'profits'.

Questions

Working through the following questions will help you to consolidate your understanding of cash flow and the other two important financial statements.

1. Work out High Note's closing Balance Sheet at the end of September. Use the information given in the example. Remember that they will have to collect £12,000 from customers; they are carrying forward £9,108 of stock, and they have 'acquired' an overdraft of £4,908.

2. Re-work the cash flow forecast for High Note, making the following revised assumptions: first, they receive£1,000 per month more cash in from customers. Second, the furniture and fittings cost £2,000 less, ie, £10,500. Your answer should provide a pleasant surprise for High Note's owner and his bankers.

3. Check if you agree with the answer to question 2, then recalculate the Profit and Loss Account for the six months' trading and the closing Balance Sheet. (Once again ignore depreciation of furniture and fixtures.)

Package of Accounts for Funds Flow Analysis at 31 December 1999 and 31 December 2000

		1999		2000
	£	£	£	£
Fixed Assets		37,340		60,340
Working Capital				
Current Assets				
Stock	19,840		29,300	
Debtors	49,460		77,600	
Cash	8,680		1,500	
	77,980		108,400	
Less Current Liabilities				
Bank Overdraft	10,000		12,000	
Creditors	48,000		58,280	
Tax	5,920		9,000	
	63,920		79,280	
Net Current Assets		14,060		29,120
Total Assets		51,400		89,460
Financed by				
Share Capital		20,000		20,000
Retained Earnings		11,400		33,460
Long-term Loan		20,000		36,000
(at 12%)		51,400		89,460

Profit and Loss Account 31 December 1999–31 December 2000

	£
Sales	672,060
Gross Profit	110,900
Expenses	75,520
Operating Profit	35,380
Loan Interest	4,320
Net Profit before Tax	31,060

Funds flow

The cash flow statement looks at the forecast movement of cash in and out of the business but, as we already know, cash is not the only money in the business. The term 'funds' is used to mean 'cash and credit', which is nearly but not quite the same as cash. From a historical point of view, a business would want to look back at the past sources and applications of funds to help predict future funding patterns.

The funds flow statement is prepared from the package of accounts. This is the opening and closing Balance Sheet, and the intervening Profit and Loss Account. Look at the example above which puts these Balance Sheets side by side, followed by a Profit and Loss Account.

Now by subtracting the opening Balance Sheet from the closing Balance Sheet and using the profit, from the Profit and Loss Account we can prepare the funds flow statement for 2000 as follows:

Sources and Applications of Funds Statement

		£
Cash and liquid funds at start of year		(1,320)
(Cash + Overdraft = £8,680 + (£10,000))		
Sources of Funds	£	
From trading ie, last year's profit before tax	31,060	
From new long-term loan	16,000	47,060
		45,740
Applications (uses of funds)	£	
Purchase of Fixed Assets	23,000	
Tax paid	5,920	

	£		
Increases in Working Capital			
Stock (29,300–19,840)	9,460		
Debtors (77,600–49,460)	28,140		
Creditors* (58,280–48,000)	(10,280)	27,320	
			£
			56,240
Cash and liquid funds at year end			(10,500)
(Cash + Overdraft = £1,500 + (£12,000))			45,740

* Creditors are people you have borrowed money from, so that has to be subtracted.

Question

Now try and answer the following question on funds flow.

4. Look at the Parkwood and Company accounts on page 58. Calculate the funds flow statement using that information.

Part 2: The Tools of Financial Analysis

Chapter 4
Business Controls

An understanding of financial reports is essential to anyone who wants to control a business, but simply knowing how these reports are constructed is not enough. To be effective, the businessman must be able to analyse and interpret that financial information.

It is highly likely that a business will want to borrow money either to get started or to expand. Bankers and other sources of finance will use specialised techniques to help them decide whether or not to invest. These techniques are the same as those used by the prudent businessman. Understanding them will help you to speak the same language as the bankers.

The starting point for any useful analysis is some appreciation of what should be happening in a given situation. If, for example, you fill your car up with petrol until it flows out, you expect the fuel gauge to read full. If it does not you would think the gauge suspect. (If you had left someone else to fill up the car you might have other doubts as well.) This would also be true for any other car you may come across.

Business objectives

There are universal methods of measuring what is happening in a business. All businesses have two fundamental objectives in common which allows us to see how well (or otherwise) they are doing.

Making a satisfactory return on investment

The first of these objectives is to make a satisfactory return (profit) on the money invested in the business.* It is hard to think

* One of the most well known returns on investment is the building society deposit rate. In recent years this has ranged between 4 and 12 per cent, so for every £100 invested, depositors received between £4 and £12 return, each year. Their capital, in this example £100, remained intact and secure.

of a sound argument against this aim. To be 'satisfactory' the return must meet four criteria:

First, it must give a fair return to shareholders, bearing in mind the risk they are taking. If the venture is highly speculative and the profits are less than building society rates, your shareholders (yourself included) will not be happy.

Second, you must make enough profit to allow the company to grow. If a business wants to expand sales it will need more working capital and eventually more space or equipment. The safest and surest source of money for this is internally generated profits, retained in the business – reserves. You will remember from the Balance Sheet that a business has three sources of new money: share capital or the owner's money; loan capital, put up by banks etc; retained profits, generated by the business.

Third, the return must be good enough to attract new investors or lenders. If investors can get a greater return on their money in some other comparable business, then that is where they will put it.

Fourth, the return must provide enough reserves to keep the real capital intact. This means that you must recognise the impact inflation has on the business. A business retaining enough profits each year to meet a 5 per cent growth in assets is actually contracting by 5 per cent if inflation is running at 10 per cent.

To control the business we have to examine carefully the various factors that affect return on investment.* Shareholders' and other lenders' funds are invested in the capital, both fixed and working, of the business, so this must be the area we relate to profitability. The example opposite shows the factors that directly influence the return on capital employed (ROCE). Capital Employed = Investment; remember the Balance Sheet must balance.

You can see that this is nothing more than a Profit and Loss Account on the left and the capital employed section of the Balance Sheet on the right. Any change that increases net profit (eg, more sales, lower expenses, less tax etc), but does not increase the amount of capital employed, will increase the ROCE percentage. Any decrease in capital employed (eg, lower stocks, fewer debtors etc), that does not lower profits, will also increase ROCE. Conversely, any change that increases capital employed without increasing profits in proportion will reduce ROCE.

---

* Return on investment is calculated in a number of different ways. The methods most suitable for a small business are covered in Chapter 5.

We shall look in detail at all the important factors that affect ROCE in Chapter 5.

Factors that affect the Return on Capital Employed (ROCE)

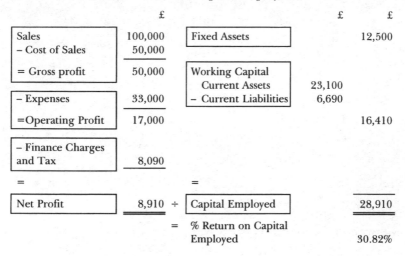

	£			£	£
Sales	100,000	Fixed Assets			12,500
– Cost of Sales	50,000				
= Gross profit	50,000	Working Capital			
		Current Assets	23,100		
– Expenses	33,000	– Current Liabilities	6,690		
=Operating Profit	17,000				16,410
– Finance Charges and Tax	8,090				
=		=			
Net Profit	8,910 ÷	Capital Employed			28,910
	=	% Return on Capital Employed			30.82%

Maintaining a sound financial position

As well as making a satisfactory return, investors, creditors and employees expect the business to be protected from unnecessary risks. Clearly, all businesses are exposed to market risks: competitors, new products and price changes are all part of a healthy commercial environment.

The sort of unnecessary risks that investors and lenders are particularly concerned about are high financial risks.

We have already seen how High Note (page 29) ran out of cash trying to make a very high return (87 per cent – £8,700 on £10,000 share capital). This was a financial risk decision, and whether taken, or stumbled into, by High Note's management, it exposed the business to the threat of liquidation.

Cash flow problems are not the only threat to a business's financial position. Heavy borrowings can bring a big interest burden to a small business. This may be acceptable when sales and profits are good, and when times are bad, shareholders can be asked to tighten their belts. Bankers, however, expect to be paid all the time. So business analysis and control are not just about profitability, but about survival and the practice of sound financial disciplines.

41

Ratios, the tools of analysis

All analysis of financial information requires comparisons. We have already seen that certain objectives are fundamental to all types of business. It is also true that there are three yardsticks against which business performance can be measured.

First, you can see how well you are meeting a personal goal. For example, you may want to double sales or add 25 per cent to profits. In a more formalised business this activity would be called budgeting, then comparisons would be made between actual results and the budget.

Second, you might want to see how well you are doing this year compared with last, comparing performance against an historical standard. This is the way in which growth in sales or profits is often measured. There are two main limitations to this sort of comparison. One rarely affects a small business and one affects all sizes of business.

If accounting methods change from year to year, perhaps in the way depreciation is dealt with, then you are not comparing like with like. Also the pounds in one year are not the same as the pounds in another, simply because inflation has changed them, so a 10 per cent growth in sales, when inflation is running at 15 per cent represents a real drop in sales volume.

Third, you may want to see how well you are doing compared with someone else's business, perhaps a competitor, or someone in a similar line of business elsewhere. This may provide useful pointers to where improvements can be made, or to new and more profitable business opportunities. For this type of analysis you need external information. Fortunately, the UK has an unrivalled wealth of readily available financial data on companies and industries. The chief sources of this information are explained in Chapter 5.

The main way in which all these business yardsticks are established is through the use of ratios. A ratio is simply something expressed as a proportion of something else, and it is intended to give an appreciation of what has happened. For example, a percentage is a particular type of ratio, where events are always compared with a base of 100.

We have already seen earlier in this chapter the return on capital employed ratio, which was expressed as a percentage. In our everyday lives we apply ratios to tell us how well, or otherwise, something is performing. One measure of a car's performance is in miles per gallon. If the mpg rate drops, say, from 35 to 1, to 20 to 1, it tells us the car is long overdue for a service – or worse. Statisticians tell us the average number of children in a family is 1.8. That is a ratio of 1.8 children to one couple.

In the financial field the opportunity for calculating ratios is great, for useful ratios, not quite so great. Chapters 5 to 7 concentrate on explaining the key ratios for a small business. Most you can calculate yourself, some you may need your book-keeper or accountant to organise for you. All take a little time and may cost a little money, but they do tell you a lot about what is going on. Derek Bok, a president of Harvard University, summed this field up nicely in the following quotation, 'If you think knowledge is expensive, try ignorance.'

The main value of financial analysis using ratios is that it points to questions that need answers. A large difference between what actually happened and what standard was set suggests that something may be wrong. The tools of analysis (the ratio covered in the next three chapters) allow managers to choose from the hundreds of questions that might be asked, the handful that are really worth answering. In a small or expanding business where time is at a considerable premium, this quick pre-selection of key questions is vital.

In the examples given in the following chapters, year end Balance Sheets and annual Profit and Loss Accounts have been used to calculate ratios. It would be more usual and useful to use monthly accounts for internal control, but for the purposes of illustration, annual figures are satisfactory.

Some problems in using ratios

Finding the information to calculate business ratios is often not the major problem. Being sure of what the ratios are really telling you almost always is.

The most common problems lie in the four following areas. (It would be very useful to read this section again, after reading the next three chapters.)

Which way is right?

There is a natural feeling with financial ratios to think that high figures are good ones, and an upward trend represents the right direction. This theory is, to some extent, encouraged by the personal feeling of wealth that having a lot of cash engenders.

Unfortunately, there is no general rule on which way is right for financial ratios. In some cases a high figure is good, in others a low figure is best. Indeed, there are even circumstances in which ratios of the same value are not as good as each other.

Look at the two working capital statements below.

Difficult Comparisons

	1.		2.	
	£	£	£	£
Current Assets				
Stock	10,000		22,990	
Debtors	13,000		100	
Cash	100	23,100	10	23,100
Less Current Liabilities				
Overdraft	5,000		90	
Creditors	1,690	6,690	6,600	6,690
Working Capital		16,410		16,410
Current Ratio*		3.4:1		3.4:1

The amount of working capital in each example is the same, £16,410, as are the current assets and current liabilities, at £23,100 and £6,690 respectively. It follows that any ratio using these factors would also be the same. For example, the current ratios in these two examples are both identical, 3.4:1, but in the first case there is a reasonable chance that some cash will come in from debtors, certainly enough to meet the modest creditor position. In the second example there is no possibility of useful amounts of cash coming in from trading, with debtors at only £100, while creditors at the relatively substantial figure of £6,600 will pose a real threat to financial stability. So in this case the current ratios are identical, but the situations being compared are not. In fact, as a general rule, a higher working capital ratio is regarded as a move in the wrong direction. The more money a business has tied up in working capital, the more difficult it is to make a satisfactory return on capital employed, simply because the larger the denominator the lower the return on capital employed.

In some cases the right direction is more obvious. A high return on capital employed is usually better than a low one, but even this situation can be a danger signal, warning that higher risks are being taken. And not all high profit ratios are good:

* The Current Ratio = Current Assets + Current Liabilities. It is explained in greater detail in Chapter 6 on Control of Working Capital.

sometimes a higher profit margin can lead to reduced sales volume and so lead to a lower ROCE.

In general, business performance as measured by ratios is best thought of as lying within a range, liquidity (current ratio), for example, staying between 1.5:1 and 2.5:1. A change in either direction represents a cause for concern.

Accounting for inflation

Financial ratios all use pounds as the basis for comparison – historical pounds at that. That would not be so bad if all these pounds were from the same date in the past, but that is not so. Comparing one year with another may not be very meaningful unless we account for the change in value of the pound.

One way of overcoming this problem is to 'adjust for inflation', perhaps using an index, such as that for consumer prices. Such indices usually take 100 as their base at some time in the past, for example, 1975. Then an index value for each subsequent year is produced showing the relative movement in the item being indexed.

The two tables below show how this could be done for High Note.

Comparing Unadjusted Ratios

Year	Sales	Sales Growth	Percentage Growth (ie, the ratio year on year)
£	£		
1	100,000	–	–
2	130,000	30,000	30
3	145,000	15,000	11.5

These unadjusted figures show a substantial growth in sales in each of the past two years.

Now if High Note's owner used a consumer price index for the appropriate time period to adjust high figures, the years could be properly compared. Let us assume that the indices for years 1, 2 and 3 were 104, 120 and 135 respectively. Year 3 is the most recent set of figures, and therefore the one we want to use as the base for comparison.

So to convert the pounds from years 1 and 2 to current pounds, we use this sum:

$$\text{Current Pounds} = \frac{\text{Index for Current Year}}{\text{Index for Historic Year}} \times \text{Historic Pounds}$$

For year 1 sales now become   135/104 × £100,000 = £129,808

          2   135/120 × £130,000 = £146,250

          3*   135/135 × £145,000 = £145,000

We can now construct an adjusted table, showing the real sales growth over the past three years.

Comparing Adjusted Ratios

Year	Adjusted Sales £	Adjusted Sales Growth £	Adjusted Growth Ratios %
1	129,808	–	–
2	146,250	16,442	12.7
3	145,000	–1,250	–0.9

The real situation is nothing like as rosy as we first thought. The sales growth in year 2 is barely a third of the original estimate. In year 3, High Note did not grow at all – in fact it contracted slightly.

The principle of this technique can be applied to any financial ratio. The appropriate index will, to some extent, depend on the nature of the business in question. To find published data, you need to look at the Annual Abstract of Statistics or the monthly Abstract of Statistics for the retail price index.

Apples and pears

There are particular problems in trying to compare one business's ratios with another. You would not expect a Mini to be able to cover a mile as quickly as a Jaguar. A small new business can achieve quite startling sales growth ratios in the early months and years. Expanding from £10,000 sales in the first six months to £50,000 in the second would not be unusual. To expect a mature business to achieve the same growth would be unrealistic. For ICI to grow from sales of £5 billion to £25 billion would imply wiping out every chemical company in the world. So some care must be taken to make sure that like is being compared with like, and allowances made for differing circumstances in the business being compared (or if the same business, the trading/economic environment of the years being compared).

* In other words, year 3 is virtually 'now'.

It is also important to check that one business's idea of an account category, say current assets, is the same as the one you want to compare it with. The concepts and principles used to prepare accounts leave some scope for differences, as Chapter 1 demonstrates.

Seasonal factors

Many of the ratios that we have looked at make use of information in the Balance Sheet. Balance Sheets are prepared at one moment in time, and may not represent the average situation. For example, seasonal factors can cause a business's sales to be particularly high once or twice a year. A Balance Sheet prepared just before one of these seasonal upturns might show very high stocks, bought in specially to meet this demand. Conversely, a look at the Balance Sheet just after the upturn might show very high cash and low stocks. If either of those stock figures were to be treated as an average it would give a false picture.

Ratios in forecasting

Ratios have another valuable use – they can be an aid to making future financial projections. For example, if you believe it prudent to hold the equivalent of a month's sales in stock, once you have made the sales forecast for future years, the projections for stock in the balance sheet follow automatically.

Questions

1. What are the two fundamental objectives that every business has in common?
2. Look back to the example of factors that can affect the return on capital employed on page 41. Assume that the gross profit will remain at a constant £50,000, whatever changes you decide to make. Recommend four changes that would increase ROCE.
3. What yardsticks could you use to measure your business's performance?
4. High Note's sales figures for the first three years have been confirmed as £100,000, £130,000 and £160,000 respectively. You also know that the consumer index for each year was 106, 124 and 140. Calculate the unadjusted sales growth ratios. Compare them with the ratios you get once you have accounted for inflation.

Chapter 5
Measures of Profitability

There are two main ways to measure a business's profitability. They are both important, but they reveal different things about the performance and perhaps even the strategy of the business. To know and understand what is happening you need information in both areas: return on capital employed and profit margins.

Return on capital employed (ROCE)

The financial resources employed in a business are called capital. We have already seen that capital can come into a business from a number of different sources. These sources have one thing in common: they all want a return – a percentage interest – on the money they invest.

There are a number of ways in which return on capital can be measured, but for a small business two are particularly important.

The ROCE ratio is calculated by expressing the profit before long-term loan interest and tax as a proportion of the total capital employed. So if you look at the High Note Profit and Loss Account on page 55 you can see that for year 1, the profit before tax is £14,850. To this we have to add the loan interest of £1,250. If we did not do this we would be double counting our cost of loan capital by expecting a return on a loan which had already paid interest. This makes the profit figure £16,100. We also ignore tax charges, not because they are unimportant or insignificant, but simply because the level of tax is largely outside the control of the business, and it is the business's performance we are trying to measure.

Now look at the balance sheet. The capital employed is the sum of the owner's capital, the profit retained and the long-term loan, in this case £28,910 (£10,000 + £8,910 + £10,000).

So the ROCE ratio for the first year is:

$$\frac{£16,100}{£28,910} = 0.56 \text{ which expressed as a percentage} = 56\%$$

The great strength of this ratio lies in the overall view it takes of the financial health of the whole business. If you look at the same ratio for the second year, you will see a small change. The ratio gives no clue as to why this has happened – it simply provides the starting point for an analysis of business performance, and an overall yardstick with which to compare absolute performance.

A banker might look to this ratio to see if the business could support more long-term borrowing (not in isolation, of course).

Return on shareholders' capital (ROSC)

The second way a small business would calculate a return on capital is by looking at the profit available for shareholders. This is not the money actually paid out, for example, as dividends, but is a measure of the increase in 'worth' of the funds invested by shareholders.

In this case the net profit after tax is divided by the owner's capital plus the retained profits (these, although not distributed, belong to the shareholders).

So in our example this would be the sum:

$$\frac{£\,8,910}{£18,910} = 0.47 \text{ which expressed as a percentage} = 47\%$$

And for the second year this ratio would be 41 per cent.

If someone was considering investing in shares in this business, then this ratio would be of particular interest to them.

Once again the difference in the ratios is clear, but the reasons are not. This is only the starting point for a more detailed analysis.

Gearing and its effects on ROSC

All businesses have access to two fundamentally different sorts of money. Equity, or owner's capital, including retained earnings, is money that is not a risk to the business. If no profits are made then the owner and other shareholders simply do not get dividends. They may not be pleased, but they cannot usually sue.

Debt capital is money borrowed by the business from outside sources; it puts the business at financial risk and is also risky for the lenders. In return for taking that risk they expect an interest payment every year, irrespective of the performance of the business.

High gearing is the name given when a business has a high proportion of outside money to inside money. High gearing has considerable attractions to a business that wants to make high returns on shareholders' capital, as the example below shows.

The effect of gearing on ROSC

		No Gearing –	Average Gearing 1:1	High Gearing 2:1	Very High Gearing 3:1
Capital Structure		£	£	£	£
Share Capital		60,000	30,000	20,000	15,000
Loan Capital (at 12%)		–	30,000	40,000	45,000
Total Capital		60,000	60,000	60,000	60,000
Profits					
Operating Profit		10,000	10,000	10,000	10,000
Less Interest on Loan		None	3,600	4,800	5,400
Net Profit		10,000	6,400	5,200	4,600
Return on Share Capital	=	10,000	6,400	5,200	4,600
		60,000	30,000	20,000	15,000
	=	16.6%	21.3%	26%	30.7%
Times Interest Earned	=	N/A	10,000	10,000	10,000
			3,600	4,800	5,400
	=	N/A	2.8X	2.1X	1.8X

In this example the business is assumed to need £60,000 capital to generate £10,000 operating profits. Four different capital structures are considered. They range from all share capital (no gearing) at one end, to nearly all loan capital at the other. The loan capital has to be 'serviced', that is, interest of 12 per cent has to be paid. The loan itself can be relatively indefinite, simply being replaced by another one at market interest rates when the first loan expires.

Following the tables through you can see that ROSC grows from 16.6 to 30.7 per cent by virtue of the changed gearing. If the interest on the loan were lower, the ROSC would be even more improved by high gearing, and the higher the interest the lower the relative improvement in ROSC. So in times of low interest, businesses tend to go for increased borrowings rather than raising more equity, that is money from shareholders.

At first sight this looks like a perpetual profit growth machine. Naturally owners would rather have someone else 'lend' them the money for their business than put it in themselves, if they could increase the return on their investment. The problem comes if the business does not produce £10,000 operating profits. Very often, in a small business, a drop in sales of 20 per cent means profits are halved. If profits were halved in this example, it could not meet the interest payments on its loan. That would make the business insolvent, and so not in a 'sound financial position'; in other words, failing to meet one of the two primary business objectives.

Bankers tend to favour 1:1 gearing as the maximum for a small business, although they have been known to go much higher. (A glance at the Laker accounts will show just how far the equation can be taken, with £200 million plus of loans to a £1 million or so equity.)

As well as looking at the gearing, lenders will study the business's capacity to pay interest. They do this by using another ratio called 'times interest earned'.

This is calculated by dividing the operating profit by the loan interest. It shows how many times the loan interest is covered, and gives the lender some idea of the safety margin. The ratio for this example is given at the end of the tables opposite. Once again rules are hard to make, but much less than 3X interest earned is unlikely to give lenders confidence.

Profit margins

Any analysis of a business must consider the current level of sales activity. If you look at High Note's P and L Accounts (page 55), you will see that materials consumed in sales have jumped from £30,000 to £43,000, a rise of 43 per cent. However, a quick look at the change in sales activity will show that the situation is nothing like so dramatic. Materials as a proportion of sales have risen from 30 to 33 per cent (30,000/100,000 = 30% and 43,000/130,000 = 33%). Obviously, the more you sell the more you must make.

To understand why there have been changes in the level of return on capital employed, we have to relate both profit and capital to sales activity. The ROCE equation can be expanded to look like this:

$$\frac{\text{Profit}}{\text{Capital}} = \frac{\text{Profit}}{\text{Sales}} \times \frac{\text{Sales}}{\text{Capital}}$$

This gives us two separate strands to examine, the profit strand and the capital strand. The first of these is usually called profit margins. The capital strand will be looked at in the next two chapters.

When we examine profit margins, all costs, expenses and the different types of profit are expressed as a percentage of sales. This ratio makes comparisons both possible and realistic.

An analysis of High Note's Profit and Loss Account will show the following changes:

Area	*Change*	*Some possible causes*
Material Cost of Sales	Up from 30% to 33%	(a) Higher prices paid (b) Change in product mix (c) Increased waste
Labour Cost of Sales	Down from 20% to 19%	(a) Reduction in wage rates (b) Increase in work rate (c) Change in product mix
Gross Profit	Down from 50% to 48%	(a) 3 per cent increase in materials (b) 1 per cent increase in labour = net 2 per cent decline in gross margin
Operating or Trading Profit	Up to 18.5% from 17%	A 3½ per cent improvement in expense ratios offset by a 2 per cent decline in gross margin = net 1½ per cent improvement in trading profit.
Net Profit before Tax	Up to 16.8% from 14.8%	Interest charges down from 2.1 per cent of sales to 1.6 per cent. Means another ½ per cent increase in net profit + 1½ per cent net increase in trading profit = 2 per cent.

Had we simply looked at the net profit margin, we would have seen a satisfactory increase, from 8.9 to 10.1 per cent. It was only by looking at each area in turn, the components of gross profit, operating or trading profit and net profit, that a useful analysis can be made. High Note's owner now has a small number of specific questions to ask in the search for reasons for changes in performance.

To summarise, the ratios of profitability that allow attention to be focused on specific areas are:

Gross profit percentage

This is deducting the cost of sales from the sales, and expressing the result as a percentage of sales.

In the High Note example for year 1 this is £100,000 (Sales) – £50,000 (Cost of Sales) = £50,000 (Gross Profit); then £50,000 (Gross Profit) + £100,000 (Sales) = 50 per cent.

This ratio gives an indication of relative manufacturing efficiency.

Operating or trading profit percentage

This is calculated by deducting expenses from the gross profit, to arrive at the operating profit. This figure is then divided by sales and expressed as a percentage. For High Note in year 1, this is £50,000 (Gross Profit) – £33,000 (Expenses) = £17,000 (Operating Profit); then £17,000 (Operating Profit) + £100,000 (Sales) = 17 per cent.

Net profit before tax percentage

In this case finance charges are deducted from operating profits to arrive at net profit before tax. This is then expressed as a percentage of sales.

For High Note, in year 1, this is £17,000 (trading Profit) – £2,150 (Interest Charge) = £14,850 (Net Profit before Tax) = 14.85 per cent.

High Note's Financial Statements
Profit and Loss Account for Years 1 and 2

	£	£	%	£	£	%
Sales		100,000	100		130,000	100
Cost of Sales						
Materials	30,000		30	43,000		33
Labour	20,000	50,000	20	25,000	68,000	19
Gross Profit		50,000	50		62,000	48
Expenses						
Rent, Rates etc	18,000			20,000		
Wages	12,000			13,000		
Advertising	3,000			3,000		
Expenses	–	33,000		2,000	38,000	
Operating or Trading Profit		17,000	17		24,000	18.5
Deduct Interest on:						
Overdraft	900					
Loan	1,250	2,150		1,250	2,050	
Net Profit before Tax		14,850	14.8		21,950	16.8
Tax Paid at 40%*		5,940			8,780	
Net Profit after Tax		8,910	8.9		13,170	10.1

Balance Sheet for Year Ends 1 and 2

Fixed Assets	£	£	£	£	£	£
Furniture and Fixtures		12,500			28,110	
Working Capital						
Current Assets						
Stock	10,000			12,000		
Debtors	13,000			13,000		
Cash	100	23,100		500	25,500	
Less Current Liabilities						
Overdraft	5,000			6,000		
Creditors	1,690	6,690		5,500	11,500	
Net Current Assets		16,410			14,000	
Capital Employed		28,910			42,110	

* Business tax rates are usually changed each year in the budget. In 1998, for example, a sole trader with profit from all activities in excess of £26,100 would pay 40 per cent tax on any profit above that level. In 1998/9, a limited company would pay corporation tax somewhere between 20 per cent and 33.5 per cent.

Financed by

Owner's Capital	10,000		18,940	
Profit Retained	8,910	18,910	13,170	32,110
Long-term Loan		10,000		10,000
Total		28,910		42,110

Taxation

The more successful a small business is, the greater its exposure to tax liabilities. Its exact tax position will depend on the legal nature of the business. A limited company will be subject to corporation tax at a set rate announced each year in the Budget. If the business is not a limited company its proprietor will be subject to income tax under Schedule D Case I or II and subject to tax rates applying to the general public.

Simply monitoring pre-tax ratios, which in themselves are satisfactory measures of trading performance only, is not enough. The owner/manager is concerned with the net profit after tax. This, after all, is the money available to help the business to grow, or to meet unforeseen problems.

Managing the tax position is one area where timely professional advice is essential. This is made even more important because tax rules change with each year's Finance Act. Good advice can both help to reduce the overall tax bill and so increase the 'worth' of profits to the business, and it can help improve cash flow by influencing the timing of tax payments. Paradoxically, business tax is being made more difficult by new taxation systems. Companies can estimate their own tax position. But they will still need advice as the responsibility for getting it right rests with them.

Reducing the tax bill

Clearly, no business plans to make losses long term but tax losses can be attractive under certain circumstances. A tax loss can occur when trading profits are 'spent' before the end of the year in question. The key question is what to spend the profits on. Obviously, whatever is bought must be of benefit to the business and the owners. The example below assumes that the owner's marginal tax rate is 40 per cent. (That is the tax band that the next sum of future income will be taxed at.)

Business A makes a trading profit of £7,500 which is declared, and tax of £3,000 is paid to the Inland Revenue. The businessman retains £4,500 of the valuable resource 'cash' (£7,500–£3,000).

Business B also makes a trading profit of £7,500, but before the year end the owner makes the following purchases:

(a) £1,300 into an approved self-employed pension scheme.
(b) A small microcomputer which costs £2,500 and will reduce dependence on an outside bureau. Remember that the Inland Revenue allows tax relief on capital expenditure over the life of the asset bought (see page 13).

Taxable profits then become £7,500 – (£1,300 + (£2,500 × 25%)) = £5,575.

Tax paid on this will be £2,230, leaving £3,345 cash.

So Business B ends up having desirable assets of 'cash' (£1,470), a pension (£1,300) and a computer (£2,500); a total of £5,270. Business B has £770 worth of assets more than Business A at the year end. This has been provided by Business B paying £770 less tax than Business A. These are only two examples of how wrong tax decisions can be made.

The Allied Dunbar Tax Guide, produced each year, provides a clear, comprehensive and up-to-date coverage of the business tax field.

Question

1. From the Parkwood accounts set out overleaf calculate the following ratios for each year:
   (a) Return on total capital employed;
   (b) Return on shareholders' capital (after tax);
   (c) Gearing;
   (d) Times interest earned;
   (e) Gross profit;
   (f) Operating profit;
   (g) Net profit after tax.

Parkwood & Co
Balance Sheet at 20 January 1999 and 2000 respectively

	£	1999 £	£	2000 £
Fixed Assets		18,670		30,170
Working Capital				
Current Assets				
Stock	9,920		14,650	
Debtors	24,730		38,800	
Cash	4,340		750	
	38,990		54,200	
Less Current Liabilities				
Bank Overdraft	5,000		6,000	
Creditors	24,000		29,140	
Tax	2,960		4,500	
	31,960		39,640	
Net Current Assets		7,030		14,560
Total Assets		25,700		44,730
Financed by				
Share Capital		10,000		10,000
Retained Earnings		5,700		16,730
Long-term loan		10,000		18,000
(at 12%)		25,700		44,730

Profit and Loss Account

	1999 £	2000 £
Sales	249,340	336,030
Cost of Goods Sold	209,450	280,580
Gross Profit	39,890	55,450
Expenses		
Sales and Marketing	10,000	15,000
Administration	10,000	20,000
General	6,668	2,760
Total Expenses	26,668	37,760
Operating Profit	13,222	17,690
Loan Interest	1,200	2,160
Net Profit before Tax	12,022	15,530
Tax due on profits	4,809	4,500
Net Profit after Tax	7,213	11,030

Chapter 6
Control of Working Capital
(or Liquidity)

The capital strand of the return on capital employed (ROCE) calculation has two main branches of its own.

$$\frac{\text{Sales}}{\text{Capital}} \text{ (ROCE)} = \frac{\text{Sales}}{\text{Fixed Assets and Working Capital}}$$

The more dynamic of these is working capital, the day-to-day money used to finance the working of the business. It is important to monitor the relationship between sales and the various elements of working capital, to see how effectively that capital is being used. But as the working capital is the difference between current assets and current liabilities, it is also important to monitor their relationship, both in total and in their component parts.

This area is very often referred to as liquidity, or the business's ability to meet its current liabilities as they fall due. The most important ratios in this area are:

The current ratio

A business's ability to meet its immediate liabilities can be estimated by relating its current assets to current liabilities. If for any reason current liabilities cannot be met, then the business is being exposed to an unacceptable level of financial risk. Suppliers may stop supplying or could even petition for bankruptcy if they are kept waiting too long for payments.

In our accounts for High Note (on page 55) the first year's picture on the Balance Sheet shows £23,100 current assets to £6,690 current liabilities.

$$\text{The Current Ratio} = \frac{\text{Current Assets}}{\text{Current Liabilities}}$$

$$\text{Therefore High Note's current ratio} = \frac{23{,}100}{6{,}690} = 3.4$$

This shows current liabilities to be covered 3.4 times, and the ratio is usually expressed in the form 3.4:1.

In the second year this has come down to 2.2:1.

At first glance this figure may look worse than the first year's position. Certainly, current liabilities have grown faster than current assets, but up to a point this is a desirable state of affairs, because it means the business is having to find less money to finance working capital.

There is really only one rule about how high (or low) the current ratio should be. It should be as close to 1:1 as the safe conduct of the business will allow. This will not be the same for every type of business.

A shop buying in finished goods on credit and selling them for cash could run safely at 1.3:1. A manufacturer, with raw material to store and customers to finance, may need over 2:1. This is because the period between paying cash out for raw materials and receiving cash in from customers is longer in a manufacturing business than in a retail business.

It is a bit like the oil dip-stick on a car. There is a band within which the oil level should be. Levels above or below that band pose different problems. So for most businesses, less than 1.2:1 would probably be cutting things a bit fine. Over 1.8:1 would mean too much cash was being tied up in such items as stocks and debtors.

An unnecessary high amount of working capital makes it harder for a business to make a good ROCE because it makes the bottom half of the sum bigger.* Too low a working capital, below 1:1 for example, exposes the business to unacceptable financial risks, eg foreclosure by banks or creditors.

The quick ratio or acid test

The quick ratio is really a belt and braces figure. In this, only assets that can be realised quickly, such as debtors and cash in hand, are related to current liabilities.

* Remember ROCE = Profit ÷ Total Capital Employed, and Total Capital = Fixed Assets + Working Capital.

$$\text{The Quick Ratio} = \frac{\text{Debtors} + \text{Cash}}{\text{Current Liabilities}}$$

For our example, looking at year one only, we would exclude the £10,000 stock because, before it can be realised, we would need to find customers to sell to and collect in the cash. All this might take several months. High Note's quick ratio would be 13,100 (cash + debtors) ÷ 6,690 (current liabilities): a perhaps too respectable 1.9:1. In the second year this has dropped to 1.2:1 (13,500 ÷ 11,500).

Once again general rules are very difficult to make, but a ratio of 0.8:1 would be acceptable for most types of business.

Credit control

Any small business selling on credit knows just how quickly customers can eat into their cash. This is particularly true if the customers are big companies. Surprisingly enough, bad debts (those which are never paid) are rarely as serious a problem as slow payers. Many companies think nothing of taking three months' credit, and it is important to remember that even if your terms are 30 days it will be nearer 45 days *on average* before you are paid. This to some extent depends on how frequently invoices are sent out. Assuming they do not go out each day – and perhaps more important, your customer *does* batch his bills for payment monthly – then that is how things will work out.

There are two techniques for monitoring debtors. The first is to prepare a schedule by 'age' of debtor. The table below gives some idea of how this might be done.

High Note's Debtors Schedule – End of Year 1

	2 months (or less) £	3 months £	4 months £	Over 4 months £	Total £
Brown & Co	1,000				
Jenkins & Son	1,000				
Andersons		3,000			
Smithers		2,500			
Thomkinsons			500		
Henry's			2,500		
Smart Inc				2,500	
	2,000	5,500	3,000	2,500	13,000

This method has the great merit of focusing attention clearly on specific problem accounts. It may seem like hard work, but once you have got the system going it will pay dividends.

The second technique for monitoring debtors is using the ratio *average collection period*.

This ratio is calculated by expressing debtors as a proportion of credit sales, and then relating that to the days in the period in question.

$$\text{Average Collection Period} = \frac{\text{Debtors}}{\text{Sales}} \times 365$$

Let us suppose that all High Note's sales are on credit and the periods in question are both 365-day years (ie, no leap years). Then in year 1 the average collection period would be:

$$\frac{£13,000 \text{ Debtors}}{£100,000 \text{ Sales}} \times 365 \text{ (days in period)} = 47 \text{ days}$$

In year 2 the collection period is:

$$\frac{£13,000 \text{ Debtors}}{£130,000 \text{ Sales}} \times 365 \text{ (days in period)} = 36 \text{ days}$$

So in the second year High Note are collecting their cash from debtors 11 days sooner than in the first year. This is obviously a better position to be in, making their relative amount of debtors lower than in year 1. It is not making the absolute amount of debtors lower, and this illustrates another great strength of using ratios to monitor performance. High Note's sales have grown by 30 per cent from £100,000 to £130,000, and their debtors have remained at £13,000.

At first glance then, their debtors are the same, neither better nor worse. But when you relate those debtors to the increased levels of sales, as this ratio does, then you can see that the position has improved.

This is a good control ratio, which has the great merit of being quickly translatable into a figure any businessman can understand, showing how much it is costing to give credit.

If, for example, High Note is paying 12 per cent for an overdraft, then giving £13,000 credit for 36 days will cost £153.86 ((12% × £13,000 × 36) ÷ 365).

Average days' credit taken

Of course, the credit world is not all one sided. Once a small business has established itself, it too will be taking credit. You can usually rely on your suppliers to keep you informed on your indebtedness – but only on an individual basis. It would be prudent to calculate how many days' credit, on average, are being taken from suppliers: a very similar sum to average collection period. The ratio is as follows:

$$\text{Average Collection Period} = \frac{\text{Creditors}}{\text{Purchases}} \times 365$$

For High Note, in year 1, this sum would be:

$$\frac{\text{£1,690 Creditors}}{\text{*£30,000 Purchases}} \times 365 \text{ (days in period)} = 21 \text{ days}$$

In year 2 this ratio would be:

$$\frac{\text{£5,500 Creditors}}{\text{£43,000 Purchases}} \times 365 \text{ (days in period)} = 47 \text{ days}$$

The difference in these ratios probably reflects High Note's greater creditworthiness in year 2. The longer the credit period you can take from your suppliers the better, provided that you still meet their terms of trade. They may, however, put you to the bottom of the list when supplies get scarce, or give you up altogether when they find a 'better' customer.

More creditor controls

There are two other useful techniques to help the owner manager keep track of these events. One is simply to relate days' credit given to days' credit taken. If they balance out then you are about even in the credit game.

In year 1, High Note gave 47 days' credit to their customers and took only 21 days from their suppliers, so they were a loser. In the second year they got ahead, giving only 36 days while taking 47.

---

* In this example it is assumed that all materials have been purchased in the period in question.

The other technique is to 'age' your creditors in exactly the same way as the debtors (see page 61). In this way it is possible to see at a glance which suppliers have been owed what sums of money, and for how long.

Stock control

Any manufacturing, subcontracting or assembling business will have to buy in raw materials and work on them to produce finished goods. They will have to keep track of three sorts of stock: raw materials, work in progress, and finished goods.

A retailing business will probably only be concerned with finished goods, and a service business may have no stocks at all.

If we assume that all High Note's stock is in finished goods, then the control ratio we can use is as follows:

$$\text{Days' finished goods stock} = \frac{\text{Finished Goods Stock}}{\text{Cost of Sales*}} \times \text{Days in period}$$

For High Note in year 1 this would be:

$$\frac{10,000}{50,000} \times 365 = 73 \text{ days}$$

In year 2 the ratio would be 64 days.

It is impossible to make any general rules about stock levels. Obviously, a business has to carry enough stock to meet customers' demand, and a retail business must have it on display or on hand. However, if High Note's supplier can always deliver within 14 days it would be unnecessary to carry 73 days' stock.

The same basic equation can be applied to both raw material and work-in-progress stock, but to reach raw materials stock you should substitute raw materials consumed for cost of sales. Once again the strength of this ratio is that a business can quickly calculate how much it is costing to carry a given level of stock, in just the same way as customer credit costs were calculated earlier.

---

* Cost of sales is used because it accurately reflects the amount of stock. The sales figure includes other items such as profit margin. If you are looking at an external company it is probable that the only figure available will be that for sales. In this case it can be used as an approximation.

Cash control

The residual element in the control of working capital is cash or, if there is no cash left, the size of overdraft needed in a particular period.

Usually the amount of cash available to a small business is finite and specific, also the size of overdraft it can take, so stock levels, creditor and debtor policies, and other working capital elements are decided with these limits in mind. This information is assembled in the cash flow forecast, which was examined in greater detail in Chapter 3.

Circulation of working capital

The primary ratio for controlling working capital is usually considered to be the current ratio. This, however, is of more interest to outside bodies, such as bankers and suppliers wanting to see how safe their money is. The manager of a business is more interested in how well the money tied up in working capital is being used.

Look at High Note's Balance Sheets for the last two years. You can see that net current assets, another name for working capital, have shrunk from £16,410 to £14,000. Not too dramatic. Now let us look at these figures in relation to the level of business activity in each year.

$$\text{Circulation of Working Capital} = \frac{\text{Sales}}{\text{Working Capital}}$$

For year 1 this is $\dfrac{100,000}{16,410} = 6X*$, and year 2 $\dfrac{130,000}{14,000} = 9X.$

So we can see that not only has High Note got less money tied up in working capital in the second year, it has also used it more efficiently. In other words, it has circulated it faster. Each pound of working capital now produces £9 of sales, as opposed to only £6 last year. And as each pound of sales makes profit, the higher the sales the higher the profit.

Averaging ratios

Ratios which involve the use of stock, debtors or creditors can be more accurately calculated by using the average of the opening

* X is a convention for 'times'.

and closing position. Seasonal factors or sales growth (contraction) will almost always make a single figure unrepresentative.

Look back to the High Note accounts on page 55. Here you can see an example where sales have grown by 30 per cent from £100,000 in the first year to £130,000 in the second. Obviously, neither the opening stock figure of £10,000, nor the closing stock of £12,000 (page 55), is truly representative of what has happened in the intervening year. It seems much more likely that the average of the opening and closing stock figures is the best figure to use in calculating the stock control ratios shown on page 64. So in this example, £11,000 (10,000 + 12,000 ÷ 2) would be the figure to use.

Questions

1. What do you understand by the term 'overtrading'?
2. Using the Parkwood accounts on page 58, calculate these ratios for both years.
   (a) The current ratio;
   (b) The quick ratio;
   (c) The average collection period (assuming all sales are on credit).
   (d) Average days' stock held (assuming all stock is finished goods);
   (e) Circulation of working capital.
3. Comment on the key changes in the ratios.

Chapter 7
Controlling Fixed Assets

A major problem that all new or expanding businesses face is exactly how much to have of such items as equipment, storage capacity and work space. New 'fixed assets' tend to be acquired in large chunks and are sometimes more opportunistic than market related in nature.

In any event, however, and for whatever reason acquired, once in the business it is important to make sure the asset is being effectively used. Controlling fixed assets splits down into two areas: looking at how effectively existing fixed assets are being used, and how to plan for new capital investments.

The fixed asset pyramid

Generally, the best way to measure how well existing fixed assets are being used is to see how many pounds' worth of sales each pound of fixed assets is generating.

The overall ratio is that of Sales ÷ Fixed Assets which gives a measure of this use of the fixed assets.

Look back to the High Note accounts on pages 55–56. The use of fixed asset ratio in that example is:

$$\text{Year 1} \quad \frac{100,000}{12,500} = 8X.^* \qquad \text{Year 2} \quad \frac{130,000}{28,110} = 4.6X.$$

This means that each pound invested in fixed assets has generated £8 worth of sales in year 1 and only £4.60 in year 2.

This 'inefficient' use of fixed assets has consumed all the benefit High Note gained from its improved use of working capital –

* X is a convention for times.

and a little more. In fact, this is the main reason why the return on capital employed (ROCE) has declined in year 2. This may be a short-term problem which will be cured when expected new sales levels are reached: not at all unusual if, for example, a new piece of machinery was bought late in the second year.

Provided the rules outlined later in this chapter on planning capital investments are followed, this problem will correct itself. Otherwise a more detailed analysis may be needed.

Looking at the overall fixed asset picture is rather like looking at the circulation of working capital ratio only as a means of monitoring working capital. There we looked at stock control, debtors and creditors as well. Fixed assets use is looked at both in total and in its component parts. A pyramid of ratios stretches out below this prime ratio.

The fixed asset pyramid will look something like this, although the nature of the assets of a particular business may suggest others be included.

The Fixed Asset Pyramid

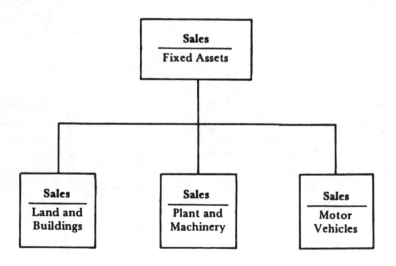

For example, a shop will also be interested in sales per square foot of selling space.

More detail still

More sophisticated businesses also monitor the output of individual pieces of equipment. They look at 'down time' (how long the equipment is out of commission), repair and maintenance costs, and the value of its output. If your business warrants it you can do this by simply expanding the pyramid as follows:

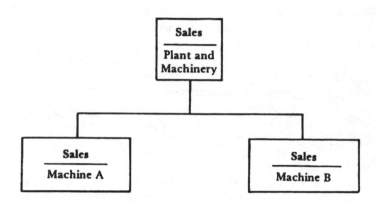

Planning new capital investment

Most businesses discover quite early on that the equipment, machinery, space etc that they started up with is not adequate for their future needs. That does not necessarily make them bad businessmen; it just shows how difficult it is to predict the future shape of any business. Perhaps they prudently chose second-hand items, or they were extremely conservative in their sales forecasts, and now simply cannot meet the demand. In any event decisions have to be taken on new investments. Should existing equipment be replaced? Should more space be acquired?

If the answer to both these questions is yes, then decisions have to be made on which equipment or space should be chosen.

It is very rare that one piece of equipment is the only absolutely correct one for the job. Suppliers compete, and most products have significant differences. They may cost more, but last longer, or cost less, but be more expensive to run.

Work space in offices and shops also comes in different shapes, sizes and locations. All these capital decisions have two things in common. They usually involve (a) spending or committing a lump sum now to get (b) a stream of benefits in the future.

Anyone buying a new piece of equipment expects it to be used to help make more products that will in turn produce cash and profits. The same argument is true if equipment is being replaced. The equipment that produces the best return should be chosen. But how will it be chosen? What tools are available to help make a sound financial choice?

Clearly it is important to try and get these decisions right. After all, these types of assets tend to be around for a long time. Also, their resale value declines rapidly in the early years. Anyone who has bought a new car will not need further emphasis on this point.

Average return on capital employed (ARCE)

We know that one of the two primary objectives of a business is to make a satisfactory return on the capital employed in the business. Clearly any new capital investment will have to achieve that same objective.

Until now we have only looked at the return on capital employed for an individual year. This would not be enough to see if a new investment proposal was worthwhile. Imagine your own reaction if someone asked you for £1,000 and explained only how they could return £200 at the end of the first year. You would expect them to come up with a complete proposal, one that covered the return of all the money you had lent – plus interest.

The same is true of any capital investment proposal. We have 'lent' the project, whatever it may be, a sum of capital. We expect a return on that capital over the working life of the assets bought. The ARCE method sets out to do just that. It measures the average profit over the life of a project and compares that with the capital employed.

Let us take an example to illustrate the method. A company is considering buying a new lathe for £5,000. The working life of the lathe will be five years, by which time it will be worthless. Net profit from the output of the lathe will come in as follows:

The ARCE Method

Year	Net Profit (after charging 100% depreciation) £
1	500
2	1,000
3	2,000
4	2,000
5	175
Total 5 years	5,675

Over the five years the capital invested in the lathe will produce an average return of £1,135 (5,675 ÷ 5) each year. As the capital concerned is £5,000 and the average return is £1,135, then the average return on the capital employed is 22.7 per cent or (1,135 ÷ 5,000) × 100.

This figure is simple to calculate and is of some help. For example, if on average the business buying the lathe is making a return of 30 per cent on capital employed, then buying the lathe will dilute the ROCE of the business as a whole.

The table below shows what happens to ROCE when the present business and the new project are 'merged' together to form the new business.

Limitations of ARCE 1

	Present Business + £	New Project £	= New Business £
Average Net Profit	6,000	1,135	7,135
Capital Employed	20,000	5,000	25,000
ROCE	30%	22.7%	28.5%

While this information is of some use as a tool for helping with capital investment decisions generally, ARCE has two severe limitations.

Let us suppose that the company has decided to buy a lathe – but there are two on offer. The first we have already examined. Profits from this lathe will build up gradually over the years and tail off sharply in the final year. The second lathe has rather different characteristics. It swings into action immediately, achieves high profits and tails off over the last three years.

Limitations of ARCE 2

Year	Net Profit from 2nd Lathe (after charging 100 per cent depreciation) £	1st Lathe Net Profit £
1	2,650	500
2	2,650	1,000
3	125	2,000
4	125	2,000
5	125	175
Totals 5 years	5,675	5,675

As the overall total profits are the same, over the five years this investment will also produce an ARCE of 22.7 per cent. And yet, if all other factors were equal and only the figures on these pages had to be considered, most businessmen would prefer the second lathe project. The reason they would give is that they get their profit in quicker. By the second year that lathe had paid for itself, while the first did not 'break even' until well into year 4.

This would be a 'gut reaction' and it would probably be right. That does not mean that 'gut reactions' are better than financial techniques; it just means we have got the wrong technique. We need a technique that takes account of when the money comes in – clearly timing matters.

This leads into average rate of return's other major failing. It uses profit as one of the measures, although a business may have to wait months and even years for that profit to be realised as cash.

The other measure it uses is the cash spent on a capital investment, so like is not being compared with like: profit on the top of the equation and cash on the bottom. Two projects could generate identical profits, but if one generated those profits in immediate cash, the ARCE technique would not recognise it. But a businessman's 'gut reaction' would once again choose the project that brought in the cash the soonest. And once again he'd be right.

Payback period

A more popular technique for evaluating capital investment decisions is the payback period method.

Payback attempts to overcome the fundamental weaknesses of the ARCE method. It compares the cash cost of the initial investment with the annual net cash inflows (or savings) that are generated by the investment. This goes beyond simply calculating profit as shown in the Profit and Loss Account, which is governed by the realisation concept. The timing of the cash movements is calculated. That is, for example, when debtors will actually pay up, and when suppliers will have to be paid. By using cash in both elements it is comparing like with like.

Payback also attempts to deal with the timing issue by measuring the time taken for the initial cost to be recovered.

The following example will illustrate the method:

The Payback Method

	£
Initial cost of project	10,000
Annual net cash inflows	
Year 1	2,000
2	4,000
3	4,000
4	2,000
5	1,000

The payment period is three years. That is when the £10,000 initial cash cost has been matched by the annual net cash inflows of £2,000, £4,000 and £4,000 of the first three years. Now we have a method that uses cash and takes some account of time.

Unfortunately it leaves us with a result that is difficult to compare directly with the profit performance of the rest of the business. If the business is currently making a 25 per cent return on capital employed, and a project has a payback period of three years, will the project enhance or reduce overall profitability? Without further calculation this question cannot be answered – and even then the answer will not necessarily be correct. Look again at the preceding example. The payback method looks only at the period taken to repay the initial investment. The following years are completely ignored, and yet the net cash inflows in those years are a benefit to the business, and their size matters.

This weakness is brought sharply into focus when competing projects are being compared.

Let us suppose your task is to choose between Projects A and B purely on financial criteria.

Limitations of Payback

	Project A £	Project B £
Initial cost of project	10,000	10,000
Annual net cash inflows		
Year 1	2,000	2,000
2	4,000	4,000
3	4,000	4,000
4	500	4,000
5	250	2,000
6	250	1,000
Total cash in flow	11,000	17,000
Payback period	3 years	3 years

The payback period for each proposal is three years, which signals that each project is equally acceptable on financial grounds. Clearly this is nonsense. It seems highly probable that Project B, which generates an extra £6,000 cash, is a better bet.

Payback has some merits, not least of which is its simplicity. It is often used as a cut-off criterion in the first stages of an evaluation. In other words, a business decides that it will not look at any project with a payback period greater than, say, four years. This provides a common starting point from which a more exacting comparison can be made. Beyond that use the method's weaknesses make it a poor tool to use in investment decisions in a small business.

Big businesses do not expect to get all their capital investment decisions right. Small businesses have to, as their very survival depends on it.

Discounted cash flow

Neither the ARCE nor payback methods for evaluating capital investment projects are wholly satisfactory. They provide neither a sound technique for deciding whether or not to invest, nor a technique to help choose between competing projects. They fail for the reasons already described, but they also fail for a more fundamental reason.

The businessman's 'gut feeling' that timing is important is perhaps more true than he thinks. No one is going to invest a pound today, unless he expects to get back more than a pound at some future date. The level of that reward if you like, is related in some way to the riskiness of the investment. But whatever the level of risk, no one wants less money back as that would involve making a loss.

The factor that alters the value of an investment over time is the interest rate. The longer the time period or the higher the interest rate the larger the final sum returned is. This relationship between the initial sum invested and the sum finally returned is familiarly known as compound interest.

The *compound interest equation* that calculates the precise figure for any interest rate or time period is:

Future Value $= £P \times (1 + r)^n$

In this equation P = the initial sum invested, or principal; r = the interest rate expressed in decimals, and n = the time period in years.

So if we invest £100 for three years at 10 per cent we can expect a future value of:

$$
\begin{aligned}
&\quad £100 \times (1 + 0.1)^3 \\
&= £100 \times (1.1)^3 \\
&= £100 \times (1.1 \times 1.1 \times 1.1) \\
&= £100 \times 1.331 \\
&= £133.10.
\end{aligned}
$$

For the doubters, the sum can be worked out in longhand.

Compound Interest Calculation

	Start £	Year 1 £	Year 2 £	Year 3 £
Balance brought forward	100.00	100.00	110.00	121.00
Interest at 10%		10.00	11.00	12.10
Value of investment	100.00	110.00	121.00	133.10
				Finish

You could consider the situation to be similar to looking through a telescope: looking forward in time through the compound interest equation magnifies the value of an investment.

But what happens when you look through the other end of a telescope? Images appear to shrink. To some extent this is similar to the problem a businessman faces when making up his mind about capital investment decisions. He knows he is not prepared to pay £1 now to get £1 back in the future. That would be bad business. What he has to calculate is exactly how much less than £1 he would pay to receive £1 back in, say, one year's time.

The thinking might go something like this. 'For this kind of investment I have to make 10 per cent profit, so I need to know what figure less 10 per cent will equal £1, and that is what I will pay now.' This is rather like moving to the other end of the telescope and looking backwards.

This problem is exactly the inverse of compounding and is called discounting. To calculate the appropriate discount factor we simply stand the compound interest equation on its head.

Discounting Calculations

$$\frac{1}{(1 + r)^n} = \frac{1}{(1 + 0.1)^1} = \frac{1}{1.1} = 0.909$$

So we would recommend that only £0.909 is paid today for £1 to be received in a year's time.

You can test the equation yourself by adding 10 per cent to £0.909. It should total £1.00.

Now we have an equation that lets us allow for the time value of money. (This is nothing whatever to do with the effects of inflation. Those effects are important and are covered later in this chapter.) Let us look at the ways to put the concept to use.

Present value

Just as the future value of an investment can be calculated using compounding, the present value of cash coming in during the years ahead can be calculated using discounting.

We have already seen the heart of the present value equation. In full, using the same symbols as for compound interest, it is:

Present Value Equation

Present Value $= £P \times \dfrac{1}{(1 + r)^n}$

The basic requirement of any present value calculation is that you have some idea of what percentage profit you want from an investment. That is not usually a very difficult problem. If you have to borrow the money at 12 per cent, pay tax on the profits and take risks as well, it is not too hard to focus on an acceptable range of interest rates.

Alternatively, the yardsticks of current returns, competitors' or industry returns, or even a personal objective, can all be used to help arrive at an acceptable cut-off interest rate for discounting. Below this cut-off rate, a project is simply not acceptable.

Look at the following example. The proposition is that you should invest £50,000 now to make £80,000 over the next five years: a clear profit of £30,000, apparently a satisfactory situation. The cash will come in and out as follows:

Cash Flow of Investment

Year	Cash out £	Cash in £	Net Cash Flow £
0	50,000	–	(50,000)
1	5,000	15,000	10,000
2	5,000	15,000	10,000
3	12,500	37,500	25,000
4	12,500	37,500	25,000
5	5,000	15,000	10,000
			30,000

This is based on a £50,000 investment now, followed by some cash expenses and cash income in the future. In other words, a typical business buying in materials, adding value and selling mainly on monthly terms. The fourth column shows the net cash flow for each year of the project's life. Cash in exceeds cash out by £30,000 – in other words the profit.

However, we know that the net cash flow received in future years is not worth as much as present pounds. Remember, no businessman will pay £1 now to receive only £1 back in the future. Our problem is to discount all the future cash flows back to present values, in exactly the same manner as we did on page 75.

Once again we could use our present value equation, but that would be rather time consuming. Fortunately there are tables that do all the sums for us, and this facility is becoming increasingly available on calculators. A set of these tables is shown on pages 91–94.

All we have to decide on now is a discount rate. Well, if we know we can have a risk-free investment of 12 per cent, it may not seem worthwhile taking a risk unless we can make 17 per cent, a modest enough figure for a risk project.

Using the discount tables we can select the appropriate year and interest rate, to arrive at the present value factor.

Present Value of Cash Flow of Investment

Year	Net Cash Flow £	Present Value Factor at 17%	Net Present Value £
0	(50,000)	1.000	(50,000)
1	10,000	0.855	8,550
2	10,000	0.731	7,310
3	25,000	0.624	15,600
4	25,000	0.534	13,350
5	10,000	0.456	4,560
			(630)

Take the present value factor for each year and multiply it by the net cash flow. This gives the net present value of the cash that this investment generates. In this case it comes to £49,370 (8,550 + 7,310 + 15,600 + 13,350 + 4,560), which is £630 less than the £50,000 we put in. So if you had expected to make 17 per cent return on your investment, you would have been disappointed.

Interestingly enough both the ARCE and payback methods would probably have encouraged you to go ahead. ARCE would have come up with average profits of £16,000 per annum, which represents a 32 per cent return on capital employed, and the payback period is 3 years and 2½ months – not long at all. But the fatal flaw in both those methods is revealed clearly by the present value concept. The timing of the cash flow over the working life of the investment is crucial, and that must form the central part of any judgement on whether to invest or not.

The profitability index

Present value is clearly a superior capital investment appraisal method, overcoming the weaknesses of the other two techniques. But in its present form it only provides the answer to our first question. Should we invest or not? Having decided on the level of return (interest) we want, and calculated the net cash flow, we simply discount to arrive at the net present value. If this is greater than zero, then the project is acceptable.

Suppose, like our problem with the lathes, the question is not simply whether to invest or not, but also to choose between alternatives, then would the present value method work? This fairly extreme example will highlight the difficulty of using the present value method alone to solve both types of problem.

Comparing Projects using the Present Value Method

Year	Project A			Project B		
	Net Cash Flow	*Present Value Factor at 10%*	*Net Present Value*	*Net Cash Flow*	*Present Value Factor at 10%*	*Net Present Value*
	£		£	£		£
0	(7,646)	1.000	(7,646)	(95,720)	1.000	(95,720)
1	3,000	0.909	2,727	30,000	0.909	27,270
2	4,000	0.826	3,304	40,000	0.826	33,040
3	5,000	0.751	3,755	50,000	0.751	37,550
	Present Value		9,786	Present Value		97,860
	Net Present Value		2,140	Net Present Value		2,140

Here we have two possible projects to invest in. One calls for capital of £7,646 and the other for £95,720. Leaving aside the problem of finding the money, which is the better investment proposition? If we are happy with making a 10 per cent return on our investment, then both projects are acceptable. Both end up with a net present value of £2,140, so that cannot be the deciding factor. Yet it is clear that A is a better bet than B, simply because the relationship between the size of the investment and the present value of the cash flow is 'better'.

The way these elements are related is through the profitability index, which is set out below:

The Profitability Index

$$\text{Profitability Index} = \frac{\text{Present Value of Earnings}}{\text{Cost of Investment}}$$

In this example the index for Project A is 128 per cent (9,786 ÷ 7,646), and for B 102 per cent (97,860 ÷ 95,720). The profitability index clearly signals that Project A is the better choice.

In fact, any comparison of projects that do not have identical initial investments and lifetimes can only be properly made using the profitability index.

To summarise then, the first step is to see if the various possible projects are acceptable by discounting their net cash flows at the cut-off interest rate. If a choice has to be made between the acceptable projects, calculate each one's profitability index, and then rank them as follows:

Project Ranking by Profitability Index

Project	Profitability Index
	%
A	135
B	127
C	117
D	104
E	101

It is not possible to have a profitability index lower than 100 per cent. That would imply a negative net present value, which in turn would eliminate the proposal at the first stage of the evaluation process.

Internal rate of return

One important piece of information has not been provided by either the net present value or the profitability index. A capital investment proposal may have a satisfactory net present value, that is a positive one, at our cut-off interest rate. It may also come out ahead of other choices in the profitability index ranking, but we still do not know exactly what rate of return we can expect to get.

This is important information for three main reasons. First, it allows us to compare new investment proposals with the rest of the business, something that neither present value nor the profitability index will do. Second, it gives us a yardstick understood by people outside the business. For example, bankers or other potential investors will understand a proposal for funds with a straightforward percentage as the end result. They will not be so sure of a figure such as £1,000 net present value. This could be misunderstood for the total profit, and be rejected. Finally, under most circumstances, the internal rate of return, as this is known, is a satisfactory method of comparing projects. (In any doubtful situations the profitability index will be the deciding factor.)

We do know, however, that the rate of return must be greater than the cut-off interest rate, provided, of course, that the net present value is positive.

This is how Project A's net present value was calculated in the profitability index example:

Calculating the Internal Rate of Return 1

Year	Net Cash Flow £	Present Value Factor at 10%	Net Present Value £
0	(7,646)	1.000	(7,646)
1	3,000	0.909	2,727
2	4,000	0.826	3,304
3	5,000	0.751	3,755
		Present Value	9,786
		Net Present Value	2140

We know that Project A is expected to make a rate of return higher than 10 per cent simply because the net present value is positive. If we increase the present value factor to, say, 20 per cent by arbitrarily raising our cut-off level, we can see whether it meets that test.

Calculating the Internal Rate of Return 2

Year	Net Cash Flow £	Present Value Factor at 20%	Net Present Value £
0	(7,646)	1.000	(7,646)
1	3,000	0.833	2,499
2	4,000	0.694	2,776
3	5,000	0.579	2,895
		Present Value	8,170
		Net Present Value	524

We can see that the project still shows a positive net present value at our new cut-off rate of 20 per cent. However, the figure is much smaller and suggests we are getting close to the 'internal rate of return'. That is the discount rate which, when applied to the net cash flow, results in a zero net present value. We could go on experimenting to reach that rate, but this would be time consuming, and not very rewarding, for reasons explained at the end of the chapter.

There is a simple technique known as interpolating, which we can use providing we have one positive and one negative net present value figure.

This is how interpolation works: let us select a discount rate that we are reasonably certain will lead to a negative net present value, for example 25 per cent.

Calculating the Internal Rate of Return 3

Year	Net Cash Flow £	Present Value Factor at 25%	Net Present Value £
0	(7,646)	1.000	(7,646)
1	3,000	0.800	2,400
2	4,000	0.640	2,560
3	5,000	0.512	2,560
		Present Value	7,520
		Net Present Value	(126)

Now we know that the internal rate of return must lie between 20 and 25 per cent. That is because the project had a positive net present value at 20 per cent and a negative one at 25 per cent. Using the interpolation equation we can arrive at a good approximation of the discount rate.

Interpolating Equation

$$\text{The Internal Rate of Return (IRR)} = \text{Lowest Trial Rate of Trial Rate} + \left[\frac{\text{Positive Cash Flow}}{\text{Range of Cash Flow}} \times \text{Difference between High and Low Rates} \right] \%$$

For this example the equation would be:

$$\text{IRR} = 20 + \left[\frac{524}{524 + 126} \times (25-20) \right] \%$$

$$= 20 + 4.03\% = 24.03\%* = 24\%.$$

Had we used the net present value figure from the 10 per cent discount calculation, we would have arrived at a different IRR. The reason is that to give an accurate IRR figure, both net present value figures used in the interpolation equation must be fairly small.

You will have an opportunity to prove both that the equation works, and that it is more accurate with low figures, at the end of the chapter.

Risk and sensitivity analysis

Discounted cash flow (DCF) gives us a sound tool for deciding whether an investment proposal is acceptable or not. It also helps

---

* It is normal practice to use only whole numbers when calculating rates of return.

us to choose between competing projects. DCF can perform one more important task: it can be used to examine the circumstances that could make a project *unacceptable*.

Look back at the second table on page 81. If the cut-off interest rate is 20 per cent this project is acceptable. The net cash flow has been calculated on a series of assumptions about sales levels, days' credit taken and given, expenses etc. But what if any one of those assumptions is wrong? For example, supposing debtors pay up much more slowly and the resultant cash flow takes longer to build up – but of course lasts longer, with some people not paying up until year 4?

The following example shows how the cash flow will look if these new 'assumptions' occur.

Sensitivity Analysis

Year	First Estimate of Net Cash Flow £	New Estimate of Net Cash Flow £	Present Value Factor at 20%	Net Present Value £
0	(7,646)	(7,646)	1.000	(7,646)
1	3,000	2,000	0.833	1,666
2	4,000	3,000	0.694	2,082
3	5,000	4,000	0.579	2,316
4		3,000	0.482	1,446
Total Positive Cash Flow	12,000	12,000	Present Value	7,510
			Net Present Value	(136)

Under these circumstances the investment would not be acceptable, so now we know how 'sensitive' the project is to customers paying up promptly. We have to assess what the risk is of these new circumstances occurring.

The same technique can be applied to any of the assumptions built into the cash flow forecast, and a good, or robust, investment proposal is one that can withstand a range of 'what if' type tests.

Dealing with inflation

A common assumption is that varying the discounted cash flow cut-off point is a good way to deal with inflation. For example, if you felt that 20 per cent was a good rate of return last year, and inflation is set to be 6 per cent next year, then 26 per cent should be the new cut-off rate.

Although attractively simple, the logic is wrong. Inflation is already dealt with in the assumptions built into the cash flow forecast (or it certainly should be). For example, the sum covering payments for materials is based on three assumptions: the volume of materials needed, how much they will cost, and when they will be paid for. The middle assumption here is where inflation is allowed for.

Discounted cash flow in working capital decisions

So far we have treated DCF as though it were exclusively for looking at investments in fixed assets. Any investment in fixed assets almost inevitably has an effect on working capital levels. DCF techniques have to be able to accommodate both fixed and working capital factors in investment decisions. Working through the following case study will show how DCF is used under these circumstances.

Launching a new product: a capital budgeting case study

Your marketing director is actively considering the launch of a new product. The following information on likely revenues and expenses has been obtained to help in the decision.

Production costs

The new product will require new equipment costing £250,000 and alterations to existing buildings and plant layout costing £120,000.

Sales forecasts and gross margins

The long range plan (LRP) for the new product expects sales to grow to £1.2m by the fifth year, with gross marketing margin running at 60 per cent.

Year	Sales Forecast (Cash) £	Cash Generated by New Product £
1	200,000	120,000
2	400,000	240,000
3	800,000	480,000
4	1,000,000	600,000
5	1,200,000	720,000

The sales of this product are not expected to eat into sales of existing products.

Marketing and sales expenses

You expect advertising and promotional expenditure to be heaviest in the first two years, tailing off to a relatively low figure later.

Promotional Expenditure

Year	£
1	150,000
2	200,000
3	100,000
4	70,000
5	50,000

Additionally, eight new sales people will be recruited to promote the product, four at the start of year 2 and the remainder at the start of year 4. Each salesperson costs the company £18,700 per annum (that includes car etc).

Debtors and stocks

These are expected to build up over the five years to a total of £220,000, about 20 per cent of sales. At the end of each year, the following amounts of extra cash will be required to finance debtors and stocks:

Year	£
1	40,000
2	40,000
3	80,000
4	40,000
5	20,000
Total investment by year 5 =	220,000

Company profit requirement

The company is unlikely to sanction a proposal generating less than 25 per cent on a DCF basis.

Case study assignment questions

1. Work out the net cash flow for each year from 0.5 inclusive.
2. Calculate the net present value (NPV) at the present 25 per cent discount rate.
3. What is the internal rate of return (IRR) of the project?

Use the worksheet provided. If you get stuck, look at the solution, which will show the logic and answer.

Launching a New Product – Worksheet

1. Annual Cash Flows

2. Cash Flow Discounted at 25%

Year		Cash Out £	Cash In £	Net Cash Flow £	Discount Rate 25% £	Discounted Cash Flow £	Discount at 20% £	Discounted Cash Flow £
0	Production				1.000		1.000	
1	Promotion							
	Debtors and Stock				0.800		0.833	
2	Promotion							
	Salesmen							
	Debtors and Stock				0.640		0.694	
3	Promotion							
	Salesmen							
	Debtors and Stock				0.512		0.579	
4	Promotion							
	Salesmen							
	Debtors and Stock				0.410		0.482	
5	Promotion							
	Salesmen							
	Debtors and Stock				0.328		0.402	

3. The Internal Rate of Return

True Rate = [   ] % =

Launching a New Product – Solution

1. Annual Cash Flows

		Cash Out £	Cash In £	Net Cash Flow £	Discount Rate 25%	Discounted Cash Flow £	Discount at 20%	Discounted Cash Flow £
0	Production	370,000	0	(370,000)	1.000	(370,000)	1.000	(370,000)
1	Promotion	150,000						
	Debtor and Stock	40,000						
		190,000	120,000	(70,000)	0.800	(56,000)	0.833	(58,310)
2	Promotion	200,000						
	Salesmen	74,800						
	Debtors and Stock	40,000						
		314,800	240,000	(74,800)	0.640	(47,872)	0.694	(51,911)
3	Promotion	100,000						
	Salesmen	74,800						
	Debtors and Stock	80,000						
		254,800	480,000	225,200	0.512	115,302	0.579	130,390
4	Promotion	70,000						
	Salesmen	149,600						
	Debtors and Stock	40,000						
		259,600	600,000	340,000	0.410	139,564	0.482	164,073
5	Promotion	50,000						
	Salesmen	149,600						
	Debtors and Stock	20,000						
		219,600	720,000	500,400	0.328	164,131	0.402	201,161
						(54,875)		15,403

2. Cash Flow Discounted at 25%

3. The Internal Rate of Return

$$\text{True Rate} = 20 + \left[\frac{15,403}{70,278} \right] \times 5 \ \% = 21.10\%$$

So don't invest if you want to make 25 per cent.

Some general factors in investment decisions

Some considerable space has been devoted to the subject of new investment appraisal. It is an area where many small businesses get into fatal problems very early on. People starting up rarely have a proper framework for deciding how much money to invest in a business idea. They are usually more concerned with how to raise the money. A critical look using discounted cash flow would probably change their minds, both about how much to spend on starting up and on expansion.

However, in the end, any investment appraisal is only as good as the information that is used to build up the cash flow forecast. Much of the benefit in using DCF is that it forces investors to think through the whole decision thoroughly.

The bulk of the work in investment appraisal is concerned with:

1. Assessment of market size, market share, market growth and selling price.
2. Estimating and phasing the initial cost of the investment; working life of facilities; working capital requirements.
3. Assessment of plant output rate.
4. Ensuring that the provision of additional services and ancillaries has not been overlooked.
5. Estimating operating costs.
6. Estimating the rate of taxation.
7. Estimating the residual value of the asset.

The relatively simple task is that of using sound investment appraisal techniques.

A general purpose DCF worksheet is provided on page 90 or use with your own projects, and the following questions.

Questions

1. Test the interpolated IRR rate of 24 per cent on page 82 to prove it is correct.
2. Use 10 per cent as the lowest trial rate in the interpolation equation on pages 81–2 to show that the nearer the net present values are to zero, the more accurate the interpolation.
3. You have to choose between the following two machines. Each has an expected life of five years and will result in net cash flows (savings) as follows:

	Machine A £	Machine B £
Cost	12,500	15,000
Net Cash Flow		
Year 1	2,000	3,000
2	4,000	6,000
3	5,000	5,000
4	2,500	3,000
5	2,000	2,000
Residual Value	1,500	2,500

To help you make your choice, calculate:

(a) The net present value of each machine at the 10 and 15 per cent discount rates.
(b) Their respective internal rates of return.
(c) Their profitability indices at the 10 per cent discount factor.

What is your choice?

General Purpose DCF Working Sheet

Time in Years from Today	Cash Outflow	Cash Inflow	Net Cash Flow	Cash flow discounted at:							
				%		%		%		%	
				Discount Factor	Present Value	Discount Factor	Present Value	Discount Factor	Present Value	Discount Factor	Present Value
	£	£	£								
0											
1											
2											
3											
4											
5											
6											
7											
8											
9											
10											
11											
12											
13											
14											
15											

Net present value

Interpolating to deduce true rate of return

$$\text{True Rate} = \text{Lowest Trial Rate} + \left[\frac{\text{Positive Cash Flow}}{\text{Range of Cash Flow}} \times \text{Difference between high and low rates} \right] \%$$

Discount tables

The present value of 1

Year					Percentage					
	1	2	3	4	5	6	7	8	9	10
1	0.990099	0.980392	0.970874	0.961538	0.952381	0.943396	0.934579	0.925926	0.917431	0.909091
2	0.980296	0.961169	0.942596	0.925556	0.907029	0.889996	0.873439	0.857339	00.841680	0.826446
3	0.970590	0.942322	0.915142	0.888996	0.863838	0.839619	0.816298	0.793832	0.772183	0.751315
4	0.960980	0.923845	0.888487	0.854804	0.822702	0.792094	0.762895	0.735030	0.708425	0.683013
5	0.951466	0.905731	0.862609	0.821927	0.783526	0.747258	0.712986	0.680583	0.649931	0.620921
6	0.942045	0.887971	0.837484	0.790315	0.746215	0.704961	0.666342	0.630170	0.596267	0.564474
7	0.932718	0.870560	0.813092	0.759918	0.710681	0.665057	0.622750	0.583490	0.547034	0.513158
8	0.923483	0.853490	0.789409	0.730690	0.676839	0.627412	0.582009	0.540269	0.501866	0.466507
9	0.914340	0.836755	0.766417	0.702587	0.644509	0.591898	0.543934	0.500249	0.460428	0.424098
10	0.905287	0.820348	0.744094	0.675564	0.613913	0.558395	0.508349	0.463193	0.422411	0.385543
11	0.896324	0.804263	0.722421	0.649581	0.584679	0.526788	0.475093	0.428883	0.387533	0.350494
12	0.887449	0.788493	0.701380	0.624597	0.556837	0.496969	0.444012	0.397114	0.355535	0.318631
13	0.878663	0.773033	0.680951	0.600574	0.530321	0.468839	0.414964	0.367698	0.326179	0.289664
14	0.869963	0.757875	0.661118	0.577475	0.505068	0.442301	0.387817	0.340461	0.299246	0.263331
15	0.861349	0.743015	0.641862	0.555265	0.481017	0.417265	0.362446	0.315242	0.274538	0.239392
16	0.852821	0.728446	0.623167	0.533908	0.458112	0.393646	0.338735	0.291890	0.251870	0.217629
17	0.844377	0.174163	0.605016	0.513373	0.436297	0.371364	0.316574	0.270269	0.231073	0.197845
18	0.836017	0.700159	0.587395	0.493628	0.415521	0.350344	0.295864	0.250249	0.211994	0.179859
19	0.827740	0.686431	0.570286	0.474642	0.395734	0.330513	0.276508	0.231712	0.194490	0.163508
20	0.819544	0.672971	0.553676	0.456387	0.376839	0.311805	0.258419	0.214548	0.178431	0.148644

| | | | | | Percentage | | | | | |
Year	11	12	13	14	15	16	17	18	19	20
1	0.900901	0.892857	0.884956	0.877193	0.869565	0.862069	0.854701	0.847458	0.840336	0.833333
2	0.811622	0.797194	0.783147	0.769468	0.756144	0.743163	0.730514	0.718184	0.706165	0.694444
3	0.731191	0.711780	0.693050	0.674972	0.657516	0.640658	0.624371	0.608631	0.593416	0.578704
4	0.658731	0.635518	0.613319	0.592080	0.571753	0.552291	0.533650	0.515789	0.498669	0.482253
5	0.593451	0.567427	0.542760	0.519369	0.497177	0.476113	0.456111	0.437109	0.419049	0.401878
6	0.534641	0.506631	0.480319	0.455587	0.432328	0.410442	0.389839	0.370432	0.352142	0.334898
7	0.481658	0.452349	0.425061	0.399637	0.375937	0.353830	0.333195	0.313925	0.295918	0.279082
8	0.433926	0.403883	0.376160	0.350559	0.326902	0.305025	0.284782	0.266038	0.248671	0.232568
9	0.390925	0.360610	0.332885	0.307508	0.284262	0.262953	0.243404	0.225456	0.208967	0.193807
10	0.352184	0.321973	0.294588	0.269744	0.247185	0.226684	0.208037	0.191064	0.175602	0.161506
11	0.317283	0.287476	0.260698	0.236617	0.214943	0.195417	0.177810	0.161919	0.147565	0.134588
12	0.285841	0.256675	0.230706	0.207559	0.186907	0.168463	0.151974	0.137220	0.124004	0.112157
13	0.257514	0.229174	0.204165	0.182069	0.162528	0.145227	0.129892	0.116288	0.104205	0.093464
14	0.231995	0.204620	0.180677	0.159710	0.141329	0.125195	0.111019	0.098549	0.087567	0.077887
15	0.209004	0.182696	0.159891	0.140096	0.122894	0.107927	0.094888	0.083516	0.073586	0.064905
16	0.188292	0.163122	0.141496	0.122892	0.106865	0.093041	0.081101	0.070776	0.061837	0.054088
17	0.169663	0.145644	0.125218	0.107800	0.092926	0.080207	0.069317	0.059980	0.051964	0.045073
18	0.152822	0.130040	0.110812	0.094561	0.080805	0.069144	0.059245	0.050830	0.043667	0.037561
19	0.137678	0.116107	0.098064	0.082948	0.070265	0.059607	0.050637	0.043077	0.036695	0.031301
20	0.124043	0.103667	0.086782	0.072762	0.061100	0.051385	0.043280	0.036506	0.030836	0.026084

Year	21	22	23	24	25	Percentage 26	27	28	29	30
1	0.826446	0.819672	0.813008	0.806452	0.800000	0.793651	0.787402	0.781250	0.775194	0.769231
2	0.683013	0.671862	0.660982	0.650364	0.640000	0.629882	0.620001	0.610352	0.600925	0.591716
3	0.564474	0.550707	0.537384	0.524487	0.512000	0.499906	0.488190	0.476837	0.465834	0.455166
4	0.466507	0.451399	0.436897	0.422974	0.409600	0.396751	0.384402	0.372529	0.361111	0.350128
5	0.385543	0.369999	0.355201	0.341108	0.327680	0.314882	0.302678	0.291038	0.279931	0.269329
6	0.318631	0.303278	0.288781	0.275087	0.262144	0.249906	0.238329	0.227374	0.217001	0.207176
7	0.263331	0.248589	0.234782	0.221844	0.209715	0.198338	0.187661	0.177636	0.168218	0.159366
8	0.217629	0.203761	0.190879	0.178907	0.167772	0.157411	0.147765	0.138778	0.130401	0.122589
9	0.179859	0.167017	0.155187	0.144280	0.134218	0.124930	0.116350	0.108420	0.101086	0.094300
10	0.148644	0.136899	0.126168	0.116354	0.107374	0.099150	0.091614	0.084703	0.078362	0.072538
11	0.122846	0.112213	0.102576	0.093834	0.085899	0.078691	0.072137	0.066174	0.060745	0.055799
12	0.101526	0.091978	0.083395	0.075673	0.068719	0.062453	0.056801	0.051699	0.047089	0.042922
13	0.083905	0.075391	0.067801	0.061026	0.054976	0.049566	0.044725	0.040390	0.036503	0.033017
14	0.069343	0.061796	0.055122	0.049215	0.043980	0.039338	0.035217	0.031554	0.028297	0.025398
15	0.057309	0.050653	0.044815	0.039689	0.035184	0.031221	0.027730	0.024652	0.021936	0.019537
16	0.047362	0.041519	0.036435	0.032008	0.028147	0.024778	0.021834	0.019259	0.017005	0.015028
17	0.039143	0.034032	0.029622	0.025813	0.022518	0.019665	0.017192	0.015046	0.013182	0.011560
18	0.032349	0.027895	0.024083	0.020817	0.018014	0.015607	0.013537	0.011755	0.010218	0.008892
19	0.026735	0.022865	0.019580	0.016788	0.014412	0.012387	0.010659	0.009184	0.007921	0.006840
20	0.022095	0.018741	0.015918	0.013538	0.011529	0.009831	0.008393	0.007175	0.006141	0.005262

| | | | | | Percentage | | | | | |
Year	31	32	33	34	35	36	37	38	39	40
1	0.763359	0.757576	0.751880	0.746269	0.740741	0.735294	0.729927	0.724638	0.719424	0.714286
2	0.582717	0.573921	0.565323	0.556917	0.548697	0.540657	0.532793	0.525100	0.517572	0.510204
3	0.444822	0.434789	0.425055	0.415610	0.406442	0.397542	0.388900	0.380507	0.372354	0.364431
4	0.339559	0.329385	0.319590	0.310156	0.301068	0.292310	0.283869	0.275730	0.267880	0.260309
5	0.259205	0.249534	0.240293	0.231460	0.223014	0.214934	0.207204	0.199804	0.192720	0.185934
6	0.197866	0.189041	0.180672	0.172731	0.165195	0.158040	0.151243	0.144786	0.138647	0.132810
7	0.151043	0.143213	0.135843	0.128904	0.122367	0.116206	0.110397	0.104917	0.099746	0.094865
8	0.115300	0.108495	0.102138	0.096197	0.090642	0.085445	0.080582	0.076027	0.071760	0.067760
9	0.088015	0.082193	0.076795	0.071789	0.067142	0.062828	0.058819	0.055092	0.051626	0.048400
10	0.067187	0.062267	0.057741	0.053574	0.049735	0.046197	0.042933	0.039922	0.037141	0.034572
11	0.051288	0.047172	0.043414	0.039980	0.036841	0.033968	0.031338	0.028929	0.026720	0.024694
12	0.039151	0.035737	0.032642	0.029836	0.027289	0.024977	0.022875	0.020963	0.019223	0.017639
13	0.029886	0.027073	0.024543	0.022266	0.020214	0.018365	0.016697	0.015190	0.013830	0.012599
14	0.022814	0.020510	0.018453	0.016616	0.014974	0.013504	0.012187	0.011008	0.009949	0.008999
15	0.017415	0.015538	0.013875	0.012400	0.011092	0.009929	0.008896	0.007977	0.007158	0.006428
16	0.013294	0.011771	0.010432	0.009254	0.008216	0.007301	0.006493	0.005780	0.005149	0.004591
17	0.010148	0.008918	0.007844	0.006906	0.006086	0.005368	0.004740	0.004188	0.003705	0.003280
18	0.007747	0.006756	0.005898	0.005154	0.004508	0.003947	0.003460	0.003035	0.002665	0.002343
19	0.005914	0.005118	0.004434	0.003846	0.003339	0.002902	0.002525	0.002199	0.001917	0.001673
20	0.004514	0.003877	0.003334	0.002870	0.002474	0.002134	0.001843	0.001594	0.001379	0.001195

Chapter 8
Costs, Volume, Pricing and Profit Decisions

In the preceding chapters we have seen how business controls can be developed. These can be used to monitor performance against the fundamental objectives of profitability, and the business's capacity to survive. So far we have taken certain decisions for granted and ignored how to cost the product or service we are marketing, and indeed, how to set the selling price. These decisions are clearly very important if you want to be sure of making a profit.

Adding up the costs

At first glance the problem is simple. You just add up all the costs and charge a bit more. The more you charge above your costs, provided the customers will keep on buying, the more profit you make.

Unfortunately as soon as you start to do the sums the problem gets a little more complex. For a start, not all costs have the same characteristics. Some costs, for example, do not change however much you sell. If you are running a shop, the rent and rates are relatively constant figures, completely independent of the volume of your sales. On the other hand, the cost of the products sold from the shop is completely dependent on volume. The more you sell the more it costs you to buy in stock.

You can't really add up those two types of costs until you have made an assumption about volume – how much you plan to sell.

	£
Rent and rates for shop	2,500
Cost of 1,000 units of volume of product	1,000
Total Costs	3,500

Look at the simple example above. Until we decide to buy, and we hope sell, 1,000 units of our product, we cannot total the costs.

With the volume hypothesised we can arrive at a cost per unit of product of:

Total Costs ÷ Number of Units
= £3,500   ÷ 1,000   = £3.50

Now provided we sell out all the above at £3.50 we shall always be profitable. But will we? Suppose we do not sell all the 1,000 units, what then? With a selling price of £4.50 we could, in theory, make a profit of £1,000 if we sell all 1,000 units. That is a total sales revenue of £4,500, minus total costs of £3,500. But if we only sell 500 units, our total revenue drops to £2,250 and we actually lose £1,250* (total revenue £2,250 − total costs £3,500). So at one level of sales a selling price of £4.50 is satisfactory, and at another it is a disaster.

This very simple example shows that all those decisions are inter-twined. Costs, sales volume, selling prices and profits are all linked together. A decision taken in any one of these areas has an impact on the other areas.

To understand the relationship between these factors, we need a picture or model of how they link up. Before we can build up this model, we need some more information on each of the component parts of cost.

The components of cost

Understanding the behaviour of costs as the trading patterns in a business change is an area of vital importance to decision makers. It is this 'dynamic' nature in every business that makes good costing decisions the key to survival. The last example showed that if the situation was static and predictable, a profit

---

* The loss may not be as dramatic as that because we may still have the product available to sell later, but if it is fresh vegetables, for example, we will not. In any event, stored products attract new costs, such as warehousing and finance charges.

was certain, but if any one component in the equation was not a certainty (in that example it was volume), then the situation was quite different.

To see how costs behave under changing conditions we first have to identify the different type of cost.

Fixed costs

Fixed costs are costs which happen, by and large, whatever the level of activity. For example, the cost of buying a car is the same whether it is driven 100 miles a year or 20,000 miles. The same is also true of the road tax, the insurance and any extras, such as a radio.

In a business, as well as the cost of buying cars, there are other fixed costs such as plant, equipment, typewriters, desks, and telephone answering machines. But certain less tangible items can also be fixed costs, for example, rent, rates, insurances etc, which are usually set quite independent of how successful or otherwise a business is.

Costs such as most of those mentioned above are fixed irrespective of the time scale under consideration. Other costs, such as those of employing people, while theoretically variable in the short term, in practice are fixed. In other words, if sales demand goes down and a business needs fewer people, the costs cannot be shed for several weeks (notice, holiday pay, redundancy etc). Also, if the people involved are highly skilled or expensive to recruit and train (or in some other way particularly valuable) and the downturn looks a short one, it may not be cost effective to reduce those short run costs in line with falling demand. So viewed over a period of weeks and months, labour is a fixed cost. Over a longer period it may not be fixed.

We could draw a simple chart showing how fixed costs behave as the 'dynamic' volume changes. The first phase of our cost model is shown overleaf.

This shows a static level of fixed costs over a particular range of output. To return to a previous example, this could show the fixed cost, rent and rates for a shop, to be constant over a wide range of sales levels.

Once the shop owner has reached a satisfactory sales and profit level in one shop, he may decide to rent another one, in which case his fixed costs will 'step' up. This can be shown in the variation on the fixed cost model overleaf.

Cost Model 1

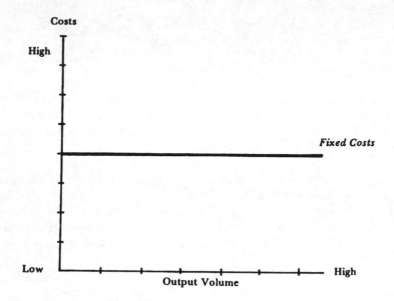

Variation on Cost Model 1

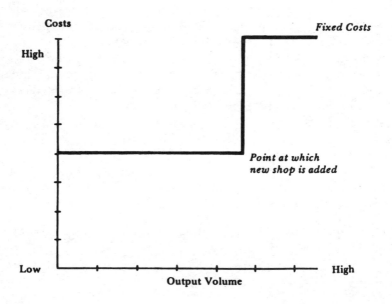

Variable costs

These are costs that change in line with output. Raw materials for production, packaging materials, bonus, piece rates, sales commission and postage are some examples. The important characteristic of a variable cost is that it rises or falls in direct proportion to any growth or decline in output volumes.

We can now draw a chart showing how variable costs behave as volume changes. The second phase of our cost model will look like this:

Cost Model 2

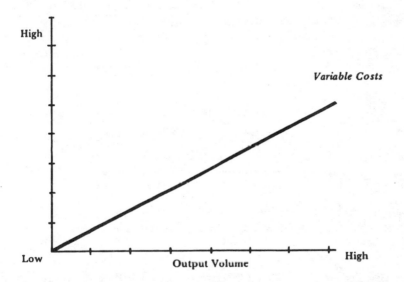

There is a popular misconception that defines fixed costs as those costs that are predictable, and variable costs as those that are subject to change at any moment. The definitions already given are the only valid ones for costing purposes.

Semi-variable costs

Unfortunately not all costs fit easily into either the fixed or variable categories.

Some costs have both a fixed and a variable element. For example, a telephone has a quarterly rental cost which is fixed, and a cost per unit consumed which is variable. In this particular example low consumers can be seriously penalised. If only a few calls are made each month, their total cost per call (fixed rental + cost per unit ÷ number of calls) can be several pounds.

Other examples of this dual component cost are photocopier rentals, electricity and gas.

These semi-variable costs must be split into their fixed and variable elements. For most small businesses this will be a fairly simple process; nevertheless it is essential to do it accurately or else much of the purpose and benefits of this method of cost analysis will be wasted.

Break-even point

Now we can bring both these phases of the costing model together to show the total costs, and how they behave.

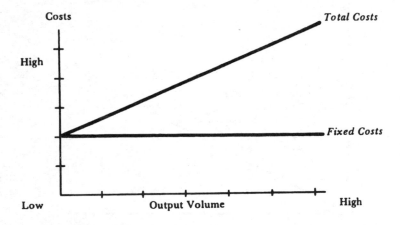

By starting the variable costs from the plateau of the fixed costs, we produce a line showing the total costs. Taking vertical and horizontal lines from any point in the total cost line will give the total costs for any chosen output volume. This is an essential feature of the costing model that lets us see how costs change with different output volumes: in other words, accommodating the dynamic nature of a business.

It is to be hoped we are not simply producing things and creating costs. We are also selling things and creating income. So a further line can be added to the model to show sales revenue as it comes in. To help bring the model to life, let's add some figures, for illustration purposes only.

100

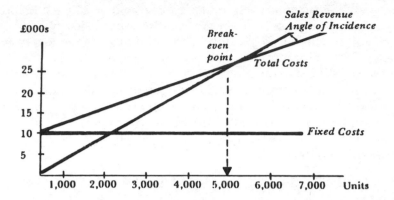

This illustration shows the break-even point (BEP). Perhaps the most important single calculation in the whole costing exercise is to find the point at which real profits start to be made.

The point where the sales revenue line crosses the total costs line is the break-even point. It is only after that point has been reached that a business can start to make profits. We can work this out by drawing a graph, such as the example above, or by using a simple formula. The advantage of using the formula as well is that you can experiment by changing the values of some of the elements in the model quickly.

The equation for BEP is:

$$\text{BEP} = \frac{\text{Fixed Costs}}{\text{Unit Selling Price} - \text{Variable Costs per Unit}}$$

This is quite logical. Before you can reach profits you must pay for the variable costs. This is done by deducting those costs from the unit selling price. What is left (usually called the unit contribution) is available to meet the fixed costs. Once enough units have been sold to meet these fixed costs, the BEP has been reached.

Let's try the sum out, given the following information shown on the break-even chart:

$$\begin{array}{rcl}
\text{Fixed Costs} &=& \text{£10,000} \\
\text{Selling Price} &=& \text{£5 per unit} \\
\text{Variable Cost} &=& \text{£3 per unit}
\end{array}$$

$$\text{So the BEP} = \frac{\text{£10,000}}{\text{£5} - \text{£3}} = \frac{\text{£10,000}}{\text{£2}} = \text{5,000 units}$$

101

Now we can see that 5,000 units must be sold at £5 each before we can start to make a profit. We can also see that if 7,000 is our maximum output we have only 2,000 units available to make our required profit target.

Obviously, the more units we have available for sale (ie, the maximum output that can realistically be sold) after our break-even point, the better. The relationship between total sales and the break-even point is called the margin of safety.

Margin of safety

This is usually expressed as a percentage and can be calculated as follows:

	£	
Total Sales	35,000	(7,000 units × £5 selling price)
Minus Break-even point	25,000	(5,000 units × £5 selling price)
Margin of safety	10,000	
Margin of safety as a Percentage of Sales	29%	(10,000 ÷ 35,000)

Clearly, the lower this percentage, the lower the business's capacity for generating profits. A low margin of safety might signal the need to rethink fixed costs, selling price or the maximum output of the business.

The angle formed at the BEP between the sales revenue line and the total cost line is called the angle of incidence. The size of the angle shows the rate at which profit is made after the break-even point. A large angle means a high rate of profit per unit sold after BEP.

Costing to meet profit objectives

By adding in the final element, desired profits, we can have a comprehensive model to help us with costing and pricing decisions.

Supposing in the previous example we knew that we had to make £10,000 profits to achieve a satisfactory return on the capital invested in the business, we could amend our BEP formula to take account of this objective:

$$\text{BEPP (Break-even Profit Point)} = \frac{\text{Fixed Costs} + \text{Profit Objective}}{\text{Unit Selling Price} - \text{Variable Costs per Unit}}$$

COSTS, VOLUME, PRICING AND PROFIT DECISIONS

Putting some figures from our last example into this equation, and choosing £10,000 as our profit objective, we can see how it works.

$$\text{BEPP} = \frac{£10,000 + £10,000}{£5 - £3} = \frac{20,000}{2} = 10,000 \text{ units}$$

Unfortunately, without further investment in fixed costs, the maximum output in our example is only 7,000 units, so unless we change something the profit objective will not be met.

The great strength of this model is that each element can be changed in turn, on an experimental basis, to arrive at a satisfactory and achievable result.

Let us return to this example. We could start our experimenting by seeing what the selling price would have to be to meet our profit objective. In this case we leave the selling price as the unknown, but we have to decide the BEP in advance (you cannot solve a single equation with more than one unknown). It would not be unreasonable to say that we would be prepared to sell our total output to meet the profit objective.

So the equation now works out as follows:

$$7,000 = \frac{20,000}{£ \text{ Unit Selling Price} - £3}$$

Moving the unknown over to the left-hand side of the equation we get:

$$£ \text{ Unit Selling Price} = \frac{£3 + 20,000}{7,000} = £3 + 2.86 = £5.86$$

We now know that with a maximum capacity of 7,000 units and a profit objective of £10,000, we have to sell at £5.86 per unit. Now if the market will stand that price then this is a satisfactory result. If it will not, then we are back to experimenting with the other variables. We must find ways of decreasing the fixed or variable costs, or increasing the output of the plant, by an amount sufficient to meet our profit objective.

Costing for special orders

Every small business is laid open to the temptation of taking a particularly big order at a 'cut-throat' price. However attractive

103

the proposition may look at first glance, certain conditions must be met before the order can be safely accepted.

Let us look at an example – a slight variation on the last one. Your company has a maximum output of 10,000 units, without any major investment in fixed costs. At present you are just not prepared to invest more money until the business has proved itself. The background information is:

Maximum output	10,000 units
Output to meet profit objective	7,000 units
Selling Price	£5.86
Fixed Costs	£10,000
Unit Variable Cost	£3.00
Profitability objective	£10,000

The break-even chart will look like this:

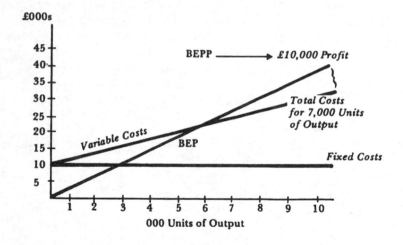

You are fairly confident that you can sell 7,000 units at £5.86 each, but that still leaves 3,000 units unsold – should you decide to produce them. Out of the blue an enquiry comes in for about 3,000 units, but you are given a strong hint that nothing less than a 33 per cent discount will clinch the deal. What should you do?

Using the costing information assembled so far, you can show the present breakdown of costs and arrive at your selling price.

Unit Cost Breakdown

	£	
Variable costs	3.00	
Contribution to fixed costs	1.43	(£10,000 fixed costs ÷ 7,000 units)
Contribution to meet profitability objective	1.43	(£10,000 profitability objective ÷ 7,000 units)
Selling price	5.86	

As all fixed costs are met on the 7,000 units sold (or to be sold), the remaining units can be sold at a price that covers both variable costs and the profitability contribution, so that you can negotiate at the same level of profitability, down to £4.43, just under 25 per cent off the current selling price. However, any selling price above the £3.00 variable cost will generate extra profits, but these sales will be at the expense of your profit margin. A lower profit margin in itself is not necessarily a bad thing if it results in a higher return on capital employed, but first you must do the sums (see Chapter 5).

There is a great danger with negotiating orders at marginal costs, as these costs are called, in that you do not achieve your break-even point soon enough and the deal results in a loss. (Look back to the first example in this chapter to see how missed sales targets affect profitability.)

Costing for business start-up

Paradoxically, one of the main reasons small businesses fail in the early stages is that too much start-up capital is used to buy fixed assets. While clearly some equipment is essential at the start, other purchases could be postponed. This may mean that 'desirable' and labour saving devices have to be borrowed or hired for a specific period. Obviously, not as nice as having them to hand all the time but if, for example, photocopiers, electronic typewriters, word processors, micros and even delivery vans are brought into the business, they become part of the fixed costs. The higher the fixed cost plateau, the longer it usually takes to reach break-even and then profitability. And time is not usually on the side of the small, new business. It has to become profitable relatively quickly or it will simply run out of money and die.

Look at these two hypothetical new small businesses. They are both making and selling identical products at the same price,

£10. They plan to sell 10,000 units each in the first year. The owner of Company A plans to get fully equipped at the start. His fixed costs will be £40,000, double that of Company B. This is largely because, as well as his own car, he has bought such things as a delivery van, new equipment and a photocopier. Much of this will not be fully used for some time, but will save some money now. This extra expenditure will result in a lower unit variable cost than Company B can achieve, a typical capital intensive result. Company B's owner, on the other hand, proposes to start up on a shoestring. Only £20,000 will go into fixed costs, but of course, his unit variable cost will be higher, at £4.50. The variable cost is higher because, for example, he has to pay an outside carrier to deliver, while A uses his own van and pays only for petrol.

Company A

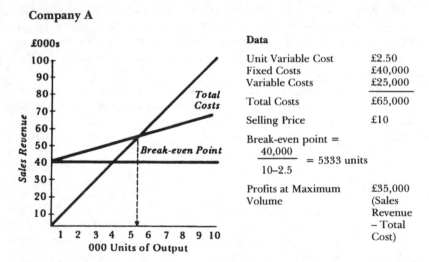

Data	
Unit Variable Cost	£2.50
Fixed Costs	£40,000
Variable Costs	£25,000
Total Costs	£65,000
Selling Price	£10

Break-even point =
$$\frac{40,000}{10-2.5} = 5333 \text{ units}$$

Profits at Maximum Volume	£35,000 (Sales Revenue – Total Cost)

The break-even chart for Company B is on page 107. From the data on each company you can see that total costs for 10,000 units are the same, so total possible profits, *if* 10,000 units are sold, are also the same. The key difference is that Company B starts making profits after 3,636 units have been sold. Company A has to wait until 5,333 units have been sold.

Now another pair of reasons why small businesses fail very early on are connected with the market place. They are frequently over-optimistic on how much they can sell. They also under-estimate how long it takes for sales to build up. So for these reasons, and spending too much start-up capital on fixed assets, great care should be taken to keep start-up fixed costs to the minimum.*

Company B

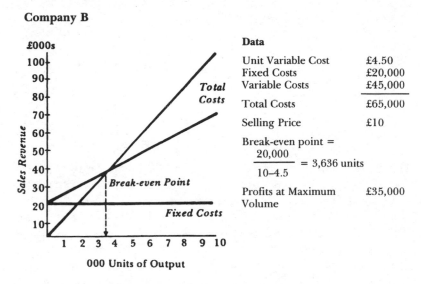

Data

Unit Variable Cost	£4.50
Fixed Costs	£20,000
Variable Costs	£45,000
Total Costs	£65,000
Selling Price	£10

Break-even point =
$$\frac{20,000}{10-4.5} = 3,636 \text{ units}$$

Profits at Maximum Volume   £35,000

Costing to eliminate unprofitable products

Not all the business's products will always be profitable. Settling down to allocate 'real' fixed costs to products can be something of an eye opener to owner-managers. Look at the example below. The business manufactures three products. Product C is bulky, complicated and a comparatively slow seller. It uses all the same sort of equipment, storage space and sales effort as products A and B, only more so. When fixed costs are allocated across the range, it draws the greatest share.

Product Profitability 1

	A £	B £	C £	Total £
Sales	30,000	50,000	20,000	100,000
Variable Costs	20,000	30,000	10,000	60,000
Allocated Fixed Costs	4,500	9,000	11,500	25,000
Total Costs	24,500	39,000	21,500	85,000
Operating Profit	5,500	11,000	(1,500)	15,000

* There are all sorts of 'persuasive' arguments to go for a capital intensive cost structure. In periods of high growth, the greater margin on sales will produce a higher ROCE, but high fixed costs will *always* expose a new or small business to higher risks. A small business has enough risks to face, with a survival rate of less than 20 per cent in its first few years, without adding to them.

This proves something of a shock. Product C is losing money, so it has to be eliminated, which will produce the following situation:

Product Profitability 2

	A £	B £	Total £
Sales	30,000	50,000	80,000
Variable Costs	20,000	30,000	50,000
New Allocated Fixed Costs	8,333	16,667	25,000
Total Costs	28,333	46,667	75,000
Operating Profit	1,667	3,333	5,000

Fixed costs will not change so the £25,000 has to be re-allocated across the remaining two products. This will result in profits dropping from £15,000 to £5,000; therefore our conventional product costing system has given the wrong signals. We have lost all the 'contribution' that Product C made to fixed costs, and any product that makes a contribution will increase overall profits. Because fixed costs cannot be ignored, it makes more sense to monitor contribution levels and to allocate costs in proportion to them.

Looking back to the first table we can see that the products made the following contributions (Contribution = Sales – Variable Costs):

Allocating Fixed Costs by Contribution Level

		Contribution £	% 	Fixed Cost Allocated £
Product	A	10,000	25	6,250
	B	20,000	50	12,500
	C	10,000	25	6,250
Total		40,000	100	25,000

Now we can re-cast the product Profit and Loss Account using this marginal costing basis.

Not only should we not eliminate Product C, but because in contribution terms it is our most profitable product, we should probably try to sell more.

Marginal Costing Product P and L Account

	A		B		C		Total
	£	%	£	%	£	%	£
Sales	30,000		50,000		20,000		100,000
Marginal Costs	20,000		30,000		10,000		60,000
Contribution	10,000	33	20,000	40	10,000	50	40,000
Fixed Costs	6,250		12,500		6,250		25,000
Product Profit	3,750	13	7,500	15	3,750	19	15,000

Questions

1. Calculate the margin of safety for Companies A and B in the example given on pages 106 and 107.
2. You are planning to start up a domestic burglar alarm business. You will be buying in the product and marketing it yourself. The main marketing effort will be a salesperson working on salary plus commission, and an advertising campaign. The financial facts are as follows (all expenses figures are for a four month period):

Item	£
Car leasing charge	1,500
Sales commission, per unit	5
Salesperson's basic salary	5,000
Rent, rates, heat, light and power	3,500
Unit buy-in price	30
Other fixed costs	4,500
Unit installation cost	10
Advertising + literature	2,000
Sundry variable costs, per unit	5
Unit selling price	100

(a) Calculate the break-even point.
(b) You decide you must have £10,000 each half year to live off. Now what unit sales do you have to achieve?
(c) You decide it is unrealistic to expect to sell more than 400 units in the first six months. What must your selling price be both to break even and make the £10,000 you need to live off?
(d) You decide to take on an installation engineer at £6,000 a half year together with another car on lease at £1,000 a half year. At the same time you increase the salesperson's salary to £8,000 and cancel the commission. Assuming that your unit selling price is once again £100, what are your answers to questions (a), (b) and (c)?

Part 3: Business Plans and Budgets

Chapter 9
Budgets

Everyone has made a budget or plan at some time. In our personal lives we are always trying to match the scarce resource 'pay', with the ever expanding range of necessities and luxuries in the market place, a battle we all too often lose, with mortgage costs, car running expenses, food and children's clothes taking more cash out than we can put in. Usually the domestic budget is confined to a periodic attempt to list and total likely future bills. These are then split into essential and non-essential items. The 'essentials' total is then deducted from expected pay (or income) and if anything is left over we can plan how to spend it.

Temporary shortages of cash are made up by taking out an overdraft, the judicious use of a credit card, or talking to a rich aunt.

Every year we review how well we have kept within our budget and moan about the unexpected expenses that always knock us off course. The usual result is that next year's pay rise just about clears the overdraft in time to start again.

Budgeting for a business

A business has to do much the same type of budgeting and planning, although much more thoroughly if it wants to survive and prosper. A business's environment is much more complex than an individual's. For example, most people have only one main source of income, and the amount of money they are likely to get in any one year is fairly easy to predict accurately. Even the smallest business has dozens or even hundreds of potential sources of income – customers – but forecasting how much they will spend is not so easy. Some small businesses start off with their plans in the owner's head or on the back of the proverbial envelope. Most of these end up going broke in the first year. (There are simply not enough 'rich aunts' to go round.)

The central problem is that to make a profit a business must take risks. A small new business must take many more risks than an established or larger one, with each risk having more important consequences if things go wrong. For example, an established firm with a thousand customers can 'afford' to lose a few to the competition. A firm with a dozen customers cannot afford to lose any.

There is no way to eliminate all risks in business. Successful entrepreneur-ship is all about anticipating the sort of risks that have to be taken, and understanding how they will affect the business. This knowledge is then used as the basis of a plan or budget. Putting this information together usually means gathering facts and opinions on the market place; interpreting their probable impact on your business; deciding what you want to happen; and finally deciding how you intend to make things happen; in other words, developing your strategy.

The small business that starts its life with a well thought through plan has great advantages over the 'seat of the pants' type of business. For a start, the plan or budget acts as a means of communicating your intentions to three vitally important audiences: the entrepreneur, the staff and the providers of finance. It is the entrepreneur's own 'dry run' before real money is put into the business and possibly lost. He can experience with various sales levels, profit margins and growth rates to arrive at a realistic picture of how he would like his business to develop, before committing himself to a particular course of action. We looked at a variation of this approach in Chapter 8 when we examined the relationship between cost/volume/profit and prices. This process will give him an invaluable insight into the mechanics of his business and help him to prepare for problems before they happen.

Also, other people working in the business will be in a better position to pull together if they know where the business is going. They can then become committed to common goals and strategies.

Bankers or shareholders outside the business will be more likely to be supportive if they see that the owner/manager knows what he wants to happen, and how to make it come about. For example, they will not be surprised by calls for cash to finance sales growth, or capital expenditure if they have seen the plans in advance.

Finally, most people who start up in business are fairly competitive. The budget acts as a standard against which they can measure their own business performance. This is particularly important for a new business in its first trading period, with no history to go on. In other words you cannot really try to do better than last year, if there wasn't one, so the only guide available is a realistic and achievable plan.

Time scale and detail

Any attempt at planning invariably begs the question, 'How far ahead should I plan?' The answer, 'As far ahead as you can usefully see', is not particularly helpful but it is the one most frequently given. Here are a few guidelines that may help bring the planning horizon into view.

Outsiders, such as bankers, may have a standard period over which they expect you to plan, if you want to borrow money from them. Usually this is at least three years, and for a new business preparing its first plan, three years is probably at the horizon itself.

The payback period, discussed in Chapter 7, is another useful concept. If it is going to take you four or five years to recover your original investment and make a satisfactory profit, then that is how far you may want to plan.

The rate of technological change is yet another yardstick used in deciding how far ahead to plan. If your business is high-tech, or substantially influenced by changes in technology, then that factor must influence your choice of planning horizon. Companies in the early stages of the computer business who looked only three years ahead would have missed all the crucial technological trends, and as technology trends are vital factors influencing the success of any business in this field, the planning time horizon must accommodate them.

The amount of detail with which you plan may also help make a long planning horizon more feasible. For example, every business should plan its first year in considerable detail. As well as a description of what the business is going to do, these plans should be summarised into month-by-month cash flow projection;* a comprehensive quarterly Profit and Loss Account; and a full opening and closing position Balance Sheet. This first year plan is usually called the budget.

---

* In a cash business such as a shop you need to project cash flow on a weekly basis.

Future years could be planned in rather less detail, giving only quarterly cash flow projection, for example. If the planning horizon is very long, plans for the final years could be confined to statements about market (and technological) trends, anticipated market share and profit margins. The detail of these plans is covered more comprehensively later in this chapter.

One final point before we look at how the budget and plans are prepared. There is a tendency to think of the budgeting process as a purely financial exercise, rather theoretical and remote from the day-to-day activity of the business. This is a serious misconception, usually fostered in larger companies, where the planners and the doers lead separate existences. People who have spent time in a large organisation have to recognise that in a small business the decision maker has to prepare his own planning. No one likes to have someone else's plans foisted upon him, a useful point to remember if a small business has a number of decision takers working in it.

In the end the budgets and plans are expressed in financial terms: cash flow forecasts, Profit and Loss Accounts and Balance Sheets. But the process of preparing the budget is firmly rooted in the real business world.

Objectives

'To the man who does not know where he is going – any road will take him there.' Every plan needs to start with a clear objective if it is to succeed. At the simplest level, for example, imagine you are planning a journey. Before you can consider whether to fly, drive, walk or take a train, you have to know your destination. You also have to know when you want to arrive and how much baggage you need with you. In other words, a clear objective. 'I want to be in Edinburgh on Thursday not later than 11 am with no more than an overnight bag.' This is a clear unambiguous objective and only now can you plan the route and the means of transport in the most effective manner.

A business also needs clear objectives to be stated before the budgeting and planning process can get under way. It needs both market and financial objectives to cover the range of its activities.

Market objectives

Sometimes referred to as the business mission or purpose, market objectives go beyond a simple statement of what product(s) you are going to sell. This mission should define precisely the market you are entering and in a way that helps you to understand the needs you are trying to satisfy. To some extent products come and go, but markets go on forever – at least the needs that the products aim to satisfy do. A simple reflection on the way in which people satisfy the need to travel will illustrate the transient nature of products. While the need to travel has grown rapidly over the past 50 years, with more people travelling more often, 'products' such as the railways and ocean liners have declined. New 'products', the motor car, the coach and the aeroplane have absorbed all the extra demand and more. (It goes without saying that this market must be compatible with your own skills and resources. A fundamental mismatch in this area would be fatal.)

For example, you may be skilled at designing and making clothes. The market place could be vast. You could concentrate on high fashion, one-off dresses, perhaps produce a range of inexpensive clothes for young girls, or you could make and market baby clothes. Each of these markets is different, and until you define your 'mission' you cannot start to plan. The following statement is the mission of one small business: 'We will design, make and market clothes for mothers-to-be that make them feel they can still be fashionably dressed.' This meets the two criteria every mission must meet.

First, it is narrow enough to give direction and guidance to everyone in the business. This concentration is the key to business success, because it is only by focusing on specific needs that a small business can differentiate itself from its larger competitors. Nothing kills off new business faster than trying to do too many different things too quickly. But the mission narrows down the task in clear steps: we are concentrating on women; this is further reduced to women at a certain stage in their lives – ie, pregnancy; this is finally reduced to those pregnant women who are fashion conscious. This is a clearly recognised need which specific products can be produced to satisfy. This is also a well-defined market that we can come to grips with.

Second, the example mission opens up a large market to allow the business to grow and realise its potential.

Interestingly enough, one of the highest incidences of failure in small businesses is in the building trade. The very nature of this field seems to mitigate against being able to concentrate on any specific type of work, or customer need. One successful new small builder defined his mission in the following sentence. 'We are going to concentrate on domestic house repair and renovation work, and as well as doing a good job we will meet the customer's two key needs: a quotation that is accurate and starting and completion dates that are met.' When told this mission, most small builders laugh. They say it cannot be done, but then most go broke.

At the end of the day, there has to be something unique about your business idea or yourself that makes people want to buy from you. That uniqueness may be confined to the fact that you are the only photocopying shop in the area, but that is enough to make you stand out (provided of course that the area has potential customers).

Also, within the market objective area you need some idea of how big you want the business to be. Your share of the market, in other words. It certainly is not easy to forecast sales, especially before you have even started trading, but if you do not set a goal at the start and you just wait and see how things develop, then one of two problems will occur. Either you will not sell enough to cover your fixed costs and you will lose money and perhaps go out of business. Or you will sell too much and run out of cash, in other words overtrade (see Chapter 3 on cash flow).

Obviously, before you can set a market share and sales objective you need to know the size of your market. We shall consider how to find that out in the next section of this chapter. Later on, when the business has been trading for a few years, it may be possible to use that sales history and experience to forecast ahead. If there are few customers then you can build up likely sales on a customer by customer basis. If there are many, then some simple mathematical technique, perhaps computer based, could be used.

But to a large extent the 'size' you want your business to be is more a judgement than a forecast, a judgement tempered by the resources you have available to achieve those objectives and, of course, some idea of what is reasonable and achievable and what is not. You will find the range of discretion over a size objective seriously constrained by the financial objectives chosen.

Profit objectives

The profit objective of every business must be to make a satisfactory return on the capital employed. We saw in Chapter 4 on business controls, that unless the return on capital employed ratio was at a certain level, a business would find it very difficult to attract outside funds. A bank manager would be fairly cool to a request for a long-term loan well below market rates. By definition 'market rates' means he could lend the money elsewhere at a rate satisfactory to him.

Another yardstick might be how much profit other people make in this type of business, even how much you could make if you invested elsewhere.

As well as making a satisfactory ROCE, the business and its profits have to grow, otherwise it will not earn enough to replace equipment or launch new products, both costly exercises. And without working equipment and a fresh product range to match the competition a business is effectively dead or dying.

So the main objectives of a new business with, say, £50,000 start-up capital, that wanted to double sales in four years, grow a little faster than the market, make a healthy and growing ROCE, and increase slightly its profit margin, might be summarised as follows:

Business Objectives

	Start-up Budget	Planning Period	4 Years On
Sales	£80,000	Details	£160,000
Profit Margin	12.5%	Omitted	13.5%
Profit	£10,000		£21,600
Capital Employed	£50,000		£86,400
ROCE	20%		25%
Market Share	5%		7%

Without a well-defined mission and clearly stated objectives a business leaves its success to chance and improvisation. (Chance leads most small businesses to fail in their first three years.)

Once we have set these primary objectives, the purpose of the budget and plans is to make sure we can achieve them. Stating the objectives provides a clear guide to future action. For example, it is obvious from the primary objectives on ROCE and profit margins that an extra £36,400 (£86,400–£50,000) of capital is needed to finance the desired sales growth over the period of the plan.

There is a school of thought that says you have to build up the plans from the market and resource appreciation, steps both described below. Then an objective can be deduced as the sum of the achievable tasks. But this exposes you to the question, 'What if this sum is not satisfactory?' It could also leave opportunity untapped. Neither of these is a very satisfactory position, so the objective's first approach, and then market appreciation, must be adopted.

Market appreciation

All businesses live or die by virtue of their success or otherwise in the market place. People very often talk of a particular market or business sector as being profitable, but without much idea of why. Years of research into the factors that influence a market's relative profitability have produced the following conclusion. 'The more intense the competition the lower the return on capital employed.' While that does not come as a great surprise in itself, it does provide some valuable pointers on how to analyse the market place. It follows that any budget or plan must be based on a sound appreciation of the competitive forces at work in a market, otherwise the primary profit objective may simply not be attainable.

For someone who has not yet started up a business, this process can act as a filter to eliminate the undesirable. For those already trading it can provide guidance on areas upon which to concentrate and on likely problem areas.

The chart below shows a way to look at these competitive forces as a whole.

Before you can start to plan in any detail you need answers to the following questions:

Where is my market? The starting point in any market appreciation has to be a definition of the scope of the market you are aiming for. A small general shop may only serve the needs of a few dozen streets. A specialist restaurant may have to call on a catchment area of 10 or 20 miles. While trends and behaviour in the wider market are helpful facts to know, your main activity is within your own area.

You may eventually decide to sell to several different markets. For example, a retail business can serve a local area through its shop and a national area by mail order. A small manufacturing business can branch out into exploring. People all too often flounder in their market research by describing their markets too broadly; for example, the motor industry, when they really mean car sales in Perth, or health foods, when they mean wholemeal bread in one small village.

Competitive Forces in a Market

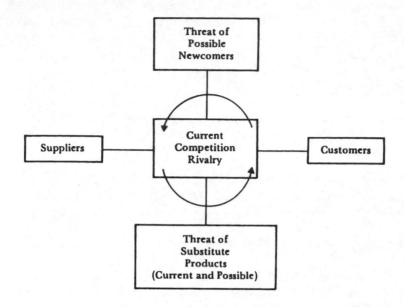

Who are the customers, potential and actual? Some products are aimed at the general public, others at particular trades or professions, males or females only, or perhaps large institutions and government departments. Some products cut across all these customer groups.

Focusing on the particular people who could buy the product gives a better idea of how many are likely to buy. Equally important, it will help you understand why they should buy from you. This really is the key to the whole business and its growth.

One entrepreneur started up a drinks vending machine business. Finding a vending machine that was reliable and easy to operate and maintain was the first task he tackled. This took two months. Next he searched for suitable ingredients ending up with a very acceptable and economic range of hot and cold drinks. He then found a finance company to lease machines to his customers. All this vital background work took nearly four months and eventually he hit the road selling. He quickly found that his potential customers were new or smallish businesses without a vending machine already, most of which were unacceptable to the leasing company because they had no financial track record. Or he had to find a large company that was on the point of changing its equip-

121

ment for one reason or another. The nature of his potential customers meant he had to call cold. (An advertising campaign using leaflets would take a long time to produce sales and he had already spent half his working capital.) He had to make something like 80 cold calls to get two interviews and it took 10 interviews to get three quotations in. Only one of those would result in an order. He ran out of cash before he could get a significant number of customers, as well as having a nervous breakdown from cold calling, a task he did not enjoy. Bringing his potential customers sharply into focus at the start and taking account of them in his business plan might have avoided this disaster.

How big is the market? You need to know this to see whether or not your sales objectives are reasonable and attainable. If there are only 1,000 possible customers for your product in the geographical market you have chosen, and five well-established competitors, then expecting to sell to 500 of them in year 1 is not on.

Is the market growing or contracting? In a growth market there are often opportunities for new companies to come in, or for small businesses to expand. In a contracting market existing competitors slog it out leaving little room for new entrants or expansion. You should find out in which direction the market is moving and at what speed. The state of the general economy may not have much bearing on the market you are in. For example, the number of video rental outlets reached their zenith in a period of economic decline in the UK.

Who are the competition and what are their strengths and weaknesses? Most products have competitors. To some extent this is reassuring because you know in advance that you are likely to achieve some sales, but you have to identify who they are and how they can affect your business. You have to know everything about them: their product range, prices, discount structure, delivery arrangements, specifications, minimum order quantities, terms of trade etc.

You also have to look at two less visible types of competitor. First, those who have not arrived on the scene yet. You have to consider what conditions would attract new businesses into the market. For example, businesses that require very little start-up capital, or add little value to goods, are always vulnerable to new competitors opening up. On the other hand, a business that can protect its ideas with patents, or achieve high volume sales quickly, is less exposed.

Second, under certain circumstances customers can be persuaded to buy a quite different or substitute product from the one you are offering, and still satisfy their same needs. In other words, you have a secondary layer of competition.

Who are the suppliers? Most businesses buy in and process raw materials of one sort or another. They add value, sell out, and make a profit. If you have only a handful of possible suppliers then they have the initiative and can set the terms of trade. For a new small business the problem is very often one of finding someone to supply in small enough volume. Nevertheless, it is a key strategic task to find at least two sources of supply for all vital products, and to negotiate the best possible deal. Otherwise the products themselves will be uncompetitive.

Forecasting sales

One of our primary market objectives is how much we would like to sell – or need to sell to achieve profit objectives. For a new business this and market share may be the only guidelines as to what sales volume could be achieved. The new business could also see what other similar ventures had achieved in their early years. However, a business with a sales history has another clue – the sales trend.

The chart below shows the quarterly sales results of a hypothetical business that has been trading for the past two years. Sales have grown from about 50 units per quarter up to just over 250 in the eight quarters.

Sales Trend

123

It is possible either mathematically or by eye to fit a trend line through these points. Continuing this trend line over the planning period shows what sales are likely to be, if the past can be accepted as a good guide to the future.

Now we can superimpose our sales objective on to a chart showing the sales trend. This will show the gap between where the business is going by virtue of its own momentum, and where we should like sales to be.

Apart from continuing our present efforts to achieve sales and sales growth, our objectives call for extra results to fill the sales gap, so within our sales operating plan specific tasks to achieve this growth have to be identified.

It is beyond the scope of this book to give more than an outline of the task involved in a market appreciation suitable for preparing a business plan. While most financial matters are common to all types of enterprise, most marketing matters are unique to a particular business.

Gap Analysis

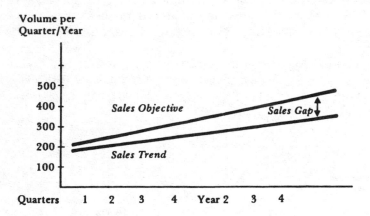

Resources appreciation

The market appreciation is a look outside the business to see the opportunities and threats to the business and its products. A business reacts to these by mobilising its resources to take advantage of the opportunities and to neutralise the threats. Business resources can be loosely grouped under four main headings: people, facilities, information and finance.

People

People, and in particular those who are vital to the success or failure of the business. Before you begin to identify specific people it is probably more important to highlight the sorts of skills and knowledge you want them to have. So the process could be summarised as a series of questions with the answers giving some guidance for future action.

Auditing your own knowledge and skills is an obvious starting point. By identifying gaps in these you can decide whom you need. The worksheet on page 127 will help to get ideas flowing.

You can then search out other people or agencies that you need to help achieve your objectives.

Facilities audit

Facilities, such as office, workshop space, storage, machinery etc, are another key source. The worksheet below can summarise the position here.

1. What fixtures, fittings, premises etc do you have or need? List.

Need	Have	Can borrow	Must find

2. What production equipment etc do you have or need? List.

Need (including some idea of output that can be achieved)	Have	Can borrow	Must find

3. Other key facilities.

You may find you already have resources you do not need. Either you put them to use or dispose of them if they cannot be pressed into service soon. They will only increase the fixed asset base of the business, tie up capital unnecessarily and make it harder to achieve your ROCE objective. (Look back at Chapter 5 to refresh your memory.)

Information audit

Information, other than pure market information, is also an important and frequently neglected resource area. Carry out an information audit.

1. What book-keeping system have you planned? Who will run it and will it give you the control you need?
2. Are there any possible legal problems related to:
   Your product or service
   Your premises
   Present or future employees
   Yourself (ie conditions in a past service contract may prevent you from working in a certain field)
   Patents etc?

Financial resource audit

Financial resources are clearly an important consideration in any planning process. They are nearly always the major constraint in any plans for a new business, whether starting up or expanding. A financial resources audit looks for answers to three questions. How much money have you got that you are prepared to commit to your business? How much do you need? Where will you get the balance from?

1. Obviously the first place to start is to find out exactly how much you have to invest in the business. You may not have much in ready cash, but you may have valuable assets that can be converted into cash, or other borrowing. The difference between your assets and liabilities is your 'net worth'. This is the maximum security that you can offer for any money borrowed and, it is to be hoped, the calculations on page 128 will yield a pleasant surprise.

Personal skills resource audit

How good are you at:

	Satisfactory	Inadequate	Person/ Help available	If not, what will you do?
MARKETING Market research Salesmanship Publicity/Advertising Product development Distribution Others (list)				
PRODUCTION Technical matters Buying Planning production Quality control Stock control Others (list)				
PEOPLE Selecting people Leading people Motivating people Team work Listening to people Giving clear instructions Others (list)				
FINANCE AND ADMINISTRATION Forming a company or partnership Finding premises Book-keeping, tax and VAT Raising money Budgeting and managing money Collecting in money Writing letters Forward planning Dealing with regulations Others (list)				

Your Net Worth

Liabilities	£	Assets	£
Overdraft		Cash in hand and in banks	
Mortgage		Building society, National Savings	
Other loans		or other deposits	
Hire purchase		Stocks and shares	
Tax due,		Current redemption value of	
including		insurance policies	
capital gains		Value of home	
Credit cards due		Any other property	
Garage, local		Motor car(s) etc	
shop accounts		Jewellery, paintings and other	
due		marketable valuables	
Any other		Any money due to you	
financial		Value of your existing business	
obligations			
Total Liabilities		Total Assets	

Net Worth = Total Assets – Total Liabilities _____

2. The sum you need to achieve your plan is calculated as follows:
   (a) First year start-up costs:

   Fixed Capital (tools, equipment, premises etc)   £

   Working Capital (materials, opening stocks,
       wages, rent, your living expenses etc)   _____

   Total Start-up Costs   _____

   (b) Additional capital to finance growth. (In the table of business objectives on page 119, item 4, the additional capital required is £36,400.)
   (c) Total capital required over planning period is the total of (a) and (b).
3. The capital you need to find is the amount by which 2 exceeds 1.

Key strategies and operating plans

So far in the budgeting and planning process we have set our business objectives, looked at market opportunities and examined our own resources. The next step is to decide what resources to commit to what market and business tasks.

Key strategies are areas of action that are vital to the success of the business. The market strategies define exactly what products/services you plan to offer to which specific customer group(s). The financial strategies explain the sources of funds and the profitability expected.

An operating plan must be made for each area of the business. For example, sales, advertising, production, equipment purchasing, raw material supplies, premises, deliveries etc. The operating plan must state the specific task to be achieved and when; what will be done, by whom and by what date. It should also monitor results. If appropriate, each task should also have an expense budget estimate against it. Your plans are complete when you have set enough tasks to achieve your primary business objectives. These plans must not be complicated, but they must be written down. They provide the backbone to the business, and the statement for others (bankers, shareholders etc) to see that you know your business direction.

An example of an operating plan is shown in the table on page 130.

People launching small businesses or trying to expand never cease to be amazed at how long their plans take to come to fruition. The much quoted rule is to estimate a time scale, double it, then double it again for good measure. The problem is that most of them simply do not think through their plans step by step, in the manner prescribed for an operating plan. Small businesses simply do not have the cash resources to allow for extensive time scales.

Contingency plans

Any plan is built on a number of assumptions. Many of these assumptions are outside the planner's control, and some are keys to the success of the venture. Look back at the earlier example of a personal objective to get to Edinburgh by a certain time (page 116). Suppose, after reviewing all the market opportunities (ie trains, planes, hire cars, buses etc) and assessing our resources (ie money, our own car etc), we decide to go by train. Unfortunately, when we get to the station we find the train has been cancelled.

A key assumption in our plan is that the train will run – but this is clearly outside our control. If by going for the train, we miss the opportunity to fly, and it is then too late to go by car or bus, we have no contingency plans; no means of achieving our objective. Now obviously in this example we could postpone going to Edinburgh, or perhaps arrive later after telephoning to explain.

Operating Plan, year ——

Planning Area	Task/Objective	Cost Budget	Time Scale	Action Required	Date	By Whom	Results of Task on Costs
Premises	Find 2,000 sq. ft. of warehouse space within five miles of workshop	£800	April–July (must be in and working by 1 August)	1. Look at area. 2. Contact estate agents a, b, c. 3. Search papers 4. Visit possible sites. 5. Review leases. 6. Sign up. 7. Take over premises.	6/5 6/5 10/5 10/6 20/6 1/7 20/7	GFK CFK GFK CFK TRD TRD GFK	
Raw material suppliers	Find two competitive suppliers of raw material 'x'	Petty cash	April–June	1. Search trade journals. 2. Write for specification and quotes 3. Chase up replies. 4. Visit four best possibles. 5. Place trial orders. 6. Select two best. 7. Place orders.	6/5 10/5 15/5 20/5 25/5 15/6 25/6	TJ TJ TJ TJ TRD TRD TJ	

But there are business situations where our objectives must be met on time, and viable contingency plans have to be prepared to make sure this happens.

For example, if a piece of production equipment breaks down, do you know where you can hire or borrow a spare quickly? Small businesses cannot afford to be out of commission for long, so contingency arrangements for all sensitive areas are essential.

The budget

Only now is it possible to construct a detailed financial picture of the business's budget and plans. This is an estimate of how the business will appear in money terms if the budget is achieved. The financial reports that summarise the effects of the operating plans are: the budgeted profit and loss; the cash flow budget; and the opening and closing balance sheets. The mechanics of preparing these financial statements have been covered in earlier chapters.

There are two further rules to be applied to the budget version of these reports, which are explained in the outline on page 132.

This example shows the sales and expenses budget broken down month by month. It is useful to divide objectives up into manageable units, rather than just leaving it until the year end to find things have gone wrong. Columns are left to report actual performance and to compare this with the budget. It is also useful to report on the year to date, which lets you see how important a particular variance is. The section at the bottom of the budget is for comments on variances and planned future action.

Do not forget at the end of the day that the business has not only to achieve its sales and profit objectives, it must also maintain a sound financial position, so working capital and debts/equity ratios (see Chapter 5) have to be carefully examined.

Budgeted P and L Account

	This Month			Year to Date		
	Budget £	Actual £	Budget Variance %	Budget £	Actual £	Budget Variance %
Sales						
Cost of Sales						
Gross Profit						
Less Expenses						
Administration						
Selling						
Marketing						
Distribution						
TOTAL						
Operating Profit						

Summary of main reasons for important variances and proposed remedial action.

1. _____

2. _____

3. _____

Budget variance analysis

One important problem can come up when variances from budget are being examined. Look at the example on page 133 which is a small part of a sales budget.

The results compared with budget, in this example, show that while sales, gross profit and net profit have high positive variances, two of the expense budgets have large adverse variances, as has cost of sales.

Normally we would expect to take corrective action to deal with adverse variances. But in this case we know that selling and distribution costs will rise directly in proportion with sales (perhaps the sales force is on commission only). So the budget variance is giving out misleading signals. Despite adverse variances being thrown up, nothing is wrong.

	Budget £	Actual £	Budget Variance	
			Value £	%
Sales	100,000	125,000	25,000	25
Cost of Sales	40,000	50,000	(10,000)	(25)
Gross Profit	60,000	75,000	15,000	25
Less Expenses				
Selling	20,000	25,000	(5,000)	(25)
Distribution	10,000	12,500	(2,500)	(25)
Marketing	5,000	5,000	–	–
Administration	5,000	5,000	–	–
Total	40,000	47,500	(7,500)	(18.75)
Operating Profit	20,000	27,500	7,500	37.5

It may be useful to express both the budget and the actual results as percentages of their respective sales figures. This allows the level of activity in the business to be taken into account as well as the actual results.

Building in Percentages

	Budget £	Ratio %	Actual £	Ratio %	Budget Variance		Ratio Variances
					Value £	%	
Sales	100,000	100	125,000	100	25,000	25	–
Cost of Sales	40,000	40	50,000	40	(10,000)	(25)	–
Gross Profit	60,000	60	75,000	60	15,000	25	–
Less Expenses							
Selling	20,000	20	25,000	20	(5,000)	(25)	–
Distribution	10,000	10	12,500	10	(2,500)	(25)	–
Marketing	5,000	5	5,000	5	–	–	–
Administration	5,000	5	5,000	5	–	–	–
TOTAL	40,000	40	47,500	40	(7,500)	(18.75)	–
Operating Profit	20,000	20	27,500	20	7,500	37.5	–

You have to be careful interpreting these percentages. An absolute rise or fall in sales or expenses may still be a 'problem', even if the ratios signal no variance. Sales shortfalls have to be made up and higher than budgeted sales have to be financed.

Flexing the sales budget

Once the annual sales volume and value figures have been set there still remains the problem of spreading them over the year.

The cash flow forecast and the budgeted P and L have to be hinged around a particular sales figure for each month. We saw in the last section the major effect that different monthly sales can have on the business's performance, both its profitability and cash flow. It is too easy to breathe a sigh of relief and just divide the annual figure by 12. This would not reflect the way we expect things to happen. In practice some periods of the year are always better than others. Even when the sales trend is generally upwards, there is an underlying seasonal pattern to every business's sales performance.

If you are preparing your first budget and plan and have no sales history to go on, then you will have to make an educated guess. You will almost certainly be able to divide the year into very slow, slow, okay, good and very good months. The pattern can be deducted by asking around other similar businesses – or potential suppliers. They will have some idea of your industry's seasonal pattern, as it will influence their own sales.

The process of spreading the annual budget over each month (or period) of the year is usually referred to as 'flexing'. If a relatively small number of customers are involved it is possible to build up a plan customer by customer, though it is doubtful if you can estimate sales to them each month, or exactly when they will buy. If you have a large number of customers then an account-by-account approach is impractical. More sophisticated businesses use mathematical forecasting techniques to calculate the underlying and seasonality factors. In a small business you have to use a rough and ready 'rule of thumb' process.

Look at the example on page 135. The left-hand column shows that we sold 108,000 units last year. Each month's actual sales are given, ranging from 9,000 units in May to 16,000 units the following April.

Now we can calculate the difference in proportion that each month's sales are from the average monthly sales. This can be done by dividing actual sales by average monthly sales. For example, for last August this proportion is $6,900 \div 9,000 = 0.77$. So despite the fact that sales generally appear to be growing, seasonal factors, such as the weather or holidays, have caused sales in August to be lower than in July or February, for example.

Month	Last Year's Sales	Sales as Proportion of Average Monthly Sales	Sales Operating Plan Average Monthly Sales	Flexed Sales Using Last Year's Proportion
May	9,000	1.00	12,000	12,000
Jun	9,000	1.00	12,000	12,000
Jul	8,900	0.99	12,000	11,880
Aug	6,900	0.77	12,000	9,240
Sep	6,900	0.77	12,000	9,240
Oct	6,500	0.72	12,000	8,640
Nov	5,300	0.59	12,000	7,080
Dec	5,800	0.64	12,000	7,680
Jan	7,000	0.78	12,000	9,360
Feb	11,700	1.30	12,000	15,600
Mar	15,000	1.67	12,000	20,000
Apr	16,000	1.78	12,000	21,300
Total Sales	108,000		144,000	144,000
Average Monthly Sales	9,000		12,000	12,000

The sales budget calls for a growth of 33½ per cent from 108,000 units to 144,000, so average monthly sales will rise from 9,000 to 12,000. Each month's sales will not be 'average', just like last year. The chances are that they will be influenced by the same seasonal factors as before.

Using the proportions already worked out we can predict what the budgeted sales should be for each month. In May, for example, the factor is 1.00 and the average sales 12,000, so the flexed sales are $1.00 \times 12,000 = 12,000$. In August the factor is 0.77, so flexed sales are $0.77 \times 12,000 = 9,240$.

You will end up with a unit sales figure for each month/period of the plan that is reasonable bearing in mind your growth objective and past seasonal experiences. This is a very rough and ready method but if you did not flex your budget and simply took an average – or average growth – you would spend the whole year either running out of cash or running out of stock.

Chapter 10
Writing and Presenting Business Plans

For most entrepreneurs the principal reason for writing up a business plan is to persuade someone to fund or partially fund their venture.

It follows, therefore, that you must give some thought as to the needs of prospective investors, and to explain how these can be accommodated when writing up and presenting your business plan.

Financiers' needs

Bankers, and indeed any other sources of debt capital, are looking for asset security to back their loan and the almost certainty of getting their money back. They will also charge an interest rate which reflects current market conditions and their view of the level of risk of the proposal. Depending on the nature of the business in question and the purpose to which the money is being used, bankers will take a 5–15 year view.

Bankers will usually expect a business to start repaying both the loan and the interest on a monthly or quarterly basis immediately the loan has been granted. In some cases a capital holiday for up to two years can be negotiated, but in the early stages of any loan the interest charges make up the lion's share of payments, like mortgage repayments.

A banker hopes the business will succeed so that he can lend more money in the future and provide more banking services, such as insurance, tax advice etc to a loyal customer.

It follows from this appreciation of a lender's needs that he is less interested in rapid growth and the consequent capital gain than he is in a steady stream of earnings almost from the outset.

As most new or fast growing businesses generally do not make immediate profits, money for such enterprises must come from elsewhere. Risk or equity capital, as other types of funds are called, comes from venture capital houses, as well as being put in by founders, their families and friends.

Because the inherent risks in investing in new and young ventures are greater than for investing in established companies, venture capital fund managers have to offer their investors the chance of larger overall returns. To do that, fund managers must not only keep failures to a minimum, they have to pick some big winners too – ventures with annual compound growth rates above 50 per cent – to offset the inevitable mediocre performers.

Typically, a fund manager would expect of any ten investments: one star, seven also-rans, and two flops.

However, it is important to remember that despite this outcome, venture capital fund managers are only looking for winners, so unless you are projecting high capital growth, the chances of getting venture capital are slim.

Not only are venture capitalists looking for winners, they are looking for a substantial shareholding in your business. There are no simple rules for what constitutes a fair split. However, *Venture Capital Report*, a UK monthly publication of investment opportunities, suggests the following starting point:

For the idea:	33 per cent
For the management:	33 per cent
For the money:	33 per cent

It all comes down to how much you need the money, how risky the venture is, how much money could be made – and your skills as a negotiator. However, it is salutary to remember that 100 per cent of nothing is still nothing, so all parties to the deal have to be satisfied if it is to succeed.

Venture capital firms may also want to put a non-executive director on the board of your company to look after their interests. Nevertheless, you will have at your disposal a talented financial brain, so be prepared to make use of him, as his services won't be free – you'll either pay up front in the fee for raising the capital, or you'll pay an annual management charge.

As fast-growing companies typically have no cash available to pay dividends, investors can only profit by selling their holdings. With this in mind the venture capitalists need to have an exit route, such as the Stock Exchange or a potential corporate buyer in view at the outset.

Unlike many entrepreneurs (and some lending bankers) who see their ventures as life-long commitments to success and growth, venture capitalists have a relatively short time horizon. Typically, they are looking to liquidate small company investments within three to seven years, allowing them to pay out individual investors and to have funds available for tomorrow's winners.

So, to be successful, your business must be targeted at the needs of these two sources of finance, and in particular at the balance between the two. Lending bankers ideally look for a ratio of £1 of debt to £1 of equity capital, but have been known to go up to £4–£5. Venture capital providers will almost always encourage entrepreneurs to take on new debt capital to match the level of equity funding.

If you are planning to raise money from friends and relatives their needs must also be taken account of in your business plan. Their funds can come in the form of debt or equity, but they may also seek some management role for themselves. Unless they have an important contribution to make, by virtue of being an accountant or marketing expert (or a respected public figure, for example) it's always best to confine their role to that of a shareholder. In that capacity they can 'give' you advice or pass on their contacts and so enhance the worth of their (and your) shareholding. But they won't hold down a post that would be better filled by someone else. Alternatively, make them a non-executive director, which may flatter them and can't harm your business. Clearly, you must use common sense in this area.

Appearance and size

The most important purpose of any written material is to create a favourable first impression. Financiers seem to have common views as to what constitutes a potentially winning business plan proposal:

- In general they want the appearance to look workmanlike. In other words, not a leatherbound book or a series of odd pages cobbled together. One partner in a major venture capital firm explained why he didn't like one entrepreneur's plan. 'This has been laid out immaculately with bookbinding and typeset pages and as a consequence it doesn't come across as a custom document assembled for targeted investors. In other words, our needs have either been ignored or treated as being identical to any other source of money. Neither of these views is particularly appealing.'

Consensus seems to favour a plastic spiral binding, holding together a pair of single colour cover sheets. This will look pleasant and be strong enough to survive being handled by a number of people.

A neat typewriter or near letter quality word processor printer will produce a satisfactory finish. Wide margins and 1.5 line spacing are also in favour, making it easier to read the plan and make notes while reading.

- Potential lenders are looking for evidence that the entrepreneur takes care over his own property and is therefore also likely to handle the investor's funds carefully. Spelling mistakes, poor grammar, typing errors and a generally untidy layout are all minus points in that respect.
- No business plan should exceed 40 pages, and most should be no longer than 20. It may be necessary to produce a separate volume of appendices, but the whole of the business arguments and funding requirements must be kept to a minimum.

Although the first draft of a business plan may be much longer than the recommended length, editing must produce a final version that fits within our target of 20–40 pages.

George Bernard Shaw is reputed to have added this postscript to a long letter sent to a friend in England: 'If I'd had more time I would have sent you a postcard.'

Layout and content

There is resistance among financial institutions to hard and fast rules on the layout and content of a business plan. This is understandable as every business and investor is different, and the standard approach taken by lawyers to wills and contracts is seen as out of place in the world of enterprise.

That being said, experience shows that certain layouts and contents have gone down better than others. These are some guidelines to producing an attractive business plan, from the investor's point of view. Not every subheading will be relevant to every type of business, but the general format should be followed, with emphasis laid as appropriate.

The cover and title page

Surprising though it may seem, a large number of business plans are submitted without any essential factual information as to how to contact the entrepreneur. They may well have written a covering letter giving some of this detail, but it is the business plan itself that gets passed around in financiers' offices.

The cover should contain the name of the company seeking funds, its address and phone number and the date on which the plan was issued. This date should confirm that this plan is the company's latest view on its position and financing needs.

The title page, immediately behind the front cover, should once again show the name and address of the company, and it should also give the chief executive's name, address and phone number. He or she is likely to be the first point of contact and anyone reading the business plan may want to talk over some aspects of the proposal before arranging a meeting.

In an upper corner, show the words 'copy number –'. This is important for at least two reasons. First, you are sending out extremely confidential information concerning your future plans, so only a limited number of copies should be in circulation and you should have a record of who has a copy.

Second, the prospective financier won't want to think he is receiving a proposal that has been hawked around the city, so a double figure number here is likely to switch him off. Remember your business plan should be targeted at specific sources of finance. It's highly likely, therefore, that you will need to assemble slightly different business plans, highlighting areas of concern to lenders as opposed to investors, for example. Each modification needs a new numbering sequence.

The executive summary

No longer than two pages, this follows immediately behind the title page. Over a third of business plans received by financiers still don't have an executive summary. A further third have one that is inadequate, inaccurate, or incomplete.

This is the most important single part of the business plan and will probably do more than anything else you do to influence whether or not the plan is reviewed in its entirety. It can also make the reader favourably disposed towards a venture at the outset, which is no bad thing.

These two pages must explain clearly and concisely:

1. The current state of the company in respect of product/service readiness for market; trading position and past successes if already running; and key staff on board.
2. The products or services to be sold and to whom they will be sold, including detail on competitive advantage.
3. The reasons customers need this product or service, together with some indication of market size and growth.
4. The company's aims and objectives both in the immediate future and two to five years ahead, and an indication of the strategies to be employed in getting there.
5. The financial forecasts, sales, profits, cash flow etc.
6. How much money is needed.
7. How and when the investor or lender will benefit from providing the funds.

This may seem a near impossible task, but it can and should be done. The three minutes or so needed to read the executive summary could be the most important in the company's entire life – either turning on, or off, a potential investor.

Obviously, the executive summary can only be written after the business plan itself has been completed.

The table of contents

After the executive summary follows a table of contents. This is the map that will guide the new readers through your business proposal and on to the 'inevitable' conclusion that he should put up the funds. If a map is obscure, muddled or even missing, the chances are you will end up with lost or even irritated readers unable to find their way around your proposal.

Each of the main sections of the business plan should be listed and the pages within that section indicated. There are two valid schools of thought on page numbering. One favours a straightforward sequential numbering of each page 1, 2, 3 ... 19, 20, for example. This seems to me to be perfectly adequate for short, simple plans, dealing with uncomplicated issues and seeking modest levels of finance.

More ambitious proposals may call for section numbering. For example, the section headed 'The Business and its Management' might be Section 1 in some business plans. In that case the pages would be identified from 1.1 to 1.8 in the table of contents, so identifying each page within that section as belonging to that specific section. Tables and figures should also bear page numbers that relate to the section in which they are found.

Individual paragraph numbering, much in favour with government and civil service departments, is considered something of an overkill in a business plan and is to be discouraged, except perhaps if you are looking for a large amount of government grant.

The table of contents on page 146 shows both the layout and content which in our experience is most in favour with financial institutions.

For the most part the remaining headings in this table of contents are reasonably self-explanatory. The financial elements of the business plan are comprehensively covered elsewhere in this book, but two areas deserve a special mention at this stage.

The deal on offer

For borrowed money the 'deal on offer' will revolve around negotiating interest rates, repayment periods and perhaps collateral and security arrangements. All relatively simple concepts covering 'easy to measure' areas of business.

For equity capital, involving the sale of a share of your business, the problems are more complex and you need to consider the following issues before preparing a deal.

How much is your business worth?

The formula used by venture capital providers to value a business is conceptually simple, but the factors used in the equation itself are somewhat subjective. The example below shows how the worth of a business can be calculated.

Example
Cranfield Engineering Ltd
Cranfield Engineering Ltd (CAL) is a new start-up business which needs a £200,000 equity injection to achieve its business plan objectives. A brief summary of its financial projections shows:

	Turnover	Profit after tax
Year 1	£200,000	(£25,000)
Year 2	£500,000	£100,000
Year 3	£750,000	£200,000

Assuming that a P/E ratio (ie the ratio of a share's price to its earnings) of 10 is used as the accepted multiplier of earnings in the industry* then using the formula:

$$\text{Present value (PV)} = \frac{\text{Future Valuation (FV)}}{(1 + i)^n}$$

where FV $\quad = $ Maintainable profits $\times$ applicable P/E ratio

and

i $\qquad\qquad = $ Required rate of return (to investor)

n $\qquad\qquad = $ Number of years until date of forecast earnings used to calculate valuation

Assuming that the figures provided by CAL are accepted at face value (which is unlikely) and that maintainable profits are achieved in year 2, and that our investor is seeking a 60 per cent return (because of the high risk involved) then the valuation of the company would be as follows:

$$PV = \frac{£(100{,}000 \times 10)}{(1 + 0.60)^2} = \frac{£1{,}000{,}000}{2.56} = £390{,}625$$

If the company is valued at £390,625 and CAL requires £200,000 then the percentage of the equity that the investor will acquire will be:

$$\frac{200{,}000}{390{,}625} \times 100 = 51.2\%$$

Obviously, while the above is mathematically correct there would be much negotiation about the acceptability of the factors being used and perhaps on which years profits represent 'maintainable profits'; in the above example, if year 3 had been used then the investor's share of the equity would have fallen to 41 per cent.

---

* For private companies the P/E ratio varies by business sector; for example bio-tech companies can be on multiples of 50 or 60, while retailers may be on 12. The stage in the economic cycle can make a difference. In 1988/89 average exit P/Es for private companies were around 10. By 1993 this had dropped to around 5.

How can you retain control?

While the equation above will show how much equity should be sold to realise a given sum of money, the business proprietor is also concerned with retaining control of the venture. It's important to realise that it is possible to retain 51 per cent of the shares. This can be done by including a restriction on voting rights in your negotiations with any potential investor. A well-known example of this A/B share type structure is the Savoy Hotel Group, in which Trusthouse Forte has the majority of the shares, some 70 per cent, but only a minority of the voting shares.

It is also important to remember that 'control' is more to do with ability, skill and entrepreneurial talent than about having the majority of shares. After all, Anita Roddick, founder of the Body Shop, Richard Branson of Virgin and Alan Sugar of Amstrad are all minority shareholders in their own companies, but no one doubts who is in control of their respective businesses.

Exit routes for outside investors

Although your time horizons may be long term and your rewards partially satisfied by non-financial things – running your own business, freedom etc – potential investors are not similarly disposed. They have their own set investment criteria, outlined above, and prior to investment they must have identified an exit route within an acceptable time scale. The most likely exit routes are:

Disposal to a trade buyer
Either you or your investor finds a larger company in a similar or complementary business and sells out to them. This is probably the No 1 exit method in terms of frequency, although it is not without its risks.

Share repurchase by entrepreneur(s)
The outside investor is bought out by the management team, usually on preferential terms, with assisted funding. This is the least popular route, commonly regarded as the option for 'also rans' which failed to match expectations.

Public share quotation
On the stock markets. While this is the less likely route, it must be the aspiration of both entrepreneur and outside investor alike. Anita Roddick of the Body Shop and Tom Farmer of Kwik-Fit are

just two of the many millionaire entrepreneurs who have taken their business to the stock market.

Sample Table of Contents

8. Financing Requirements

9. Business Controls

Appendices could include:
    Management team biographies
    Names and details of professional advisers
    Technical data and drawings
    Details of patents, copyright, designs
    Post audited accounts
    Consultants' reports, or other published data
      on products, markets etc
    Orders on hand and enquiry status
    Detailed market research methods and findings
    Organisation charts

NB. Additional separate entries for tables and figures should be provided using the same page numbering method, eg: Competitor Data, Table 1, page 3.7 etc.

Writing and editing

The first draft of your business plan should be written by yourself and your management team. Each person involved should write up the part of the plan for which he is directly responsible, eg the production director writes up 'manufacturing' and the sales director 'selling'. Each section should then be circulated for comments and criticisms. This is usually the moment when tempers flare, but it is also the point where the managing director can exercise his talents for smoothing ruffled feathers and welding a group of people, pulling in different directions, into a coherent team.

Don't worry too much that each section has been written in a different style; this and other matters of presentation can be dealt with later.

Once the first draft of the business plan has been agreed, it should be submitted to the firm's professional advisers. Lawyers and accountants have considerable experience in dealing with investors, bankers and the Stock Exchange, so they will know how best to present the facts you have assembled. They will also advise on the appropriate language to be used when making statements example, that investors will receive a return of at least 100 per cent annually on their investment could result in an unwelcome visit from G7 (the Fraud Squad) if forecasts are not subsequently achieved.

This would also be a good time to talk the proposal over with a 'friendly' banker or venture capital provider. He can give an insider's view as to what needs beefing up or playing down.

After the first draft of the business plan has been reviewed by the management team and their professional advisers comes the task of moulding it into a readable document that prospective investors will find attractive. This will call for a professional examination of such matters as: syntax, grammar, spelling, consistency, clarity, elimination of jargon and repetition and the business plan's overall organisation. There is absolutely no doubt that a well-written business plan is better received than one that is poorly written, so take advice. Freelance business journalists, editors of trade magazines, regional journalists, English teachers, librarians and professional freelance editors are all people accustomed to simplifying and organising language and expressing ideas in a way that will keep their audience's interest.

Before any business plan is sent out to any prospective investor or lender, it should be carefully proofread – misspellings and typing mistakes carry a strong negative message to financiers.

Who to send it to

Now you are ready to send out your business plan to a few carefully selected financial institutions who you know are interested in proposals such as yours. The British Venture Capital Association (address page 172) has over 200 member-organisations that are involved in the provision of venture capital. A list of these members, together with useful details such as members' investment and industry preferences, is published annually as the *BVCA Directory*. The BVCA also publishes *A Directory of Business Introduction Services*, linking entrepreneurs to business angels within the UK.

This will involve some research into the particular interests, foibles and idiosyncrasies of the institutions themselves. If you are only interested in raising Dept capital, the field is narrowed to the clearing banks, for the main part. If you are looking for someone to share the risk with you, you must review the much wider field of venture capital. Here some institutions will only look at proposals over a certain capital sum, such as £250,000, or will only invest in certain technologies.

It would be as well to carry out this research before the final editing of your business plan, as you should incorporate something of this knowledge in the way your business plan is presented. You may well find that slightly different versions of Section 8.5 'The deal on offer' have to be made up for each different source or finance to which you send your business plan.

Finally, how long will it all take? This also depends on whether you are raising debt or equity, the institution you approach and the complexity of the deal on offer. A secured bank loan, for example, can take from a few days to a few weeks to arrange.

Investment from a venture capital house will rarely take less than three months to arrange, more usually take six, and could even take up to nine. Though the deal itself may be struck early on, the lawyers will pore over the detail for weeks. Every exchange of letters can add a fortnight to the wait. So timing is another factor to consider when deciding who to send your plan to and what sort of finance to raise – and the timing will have to be allowed for in your projections.

The oral presentation

If getting someone interested in your business plan is half the battle in raising funds, the other half is the oral presentation. Any organisation financing a venture will insist on seeing the team involved presenting and defending their plans – in person. They know that they are backing people every bit as much as the idea, and you need to have that fact in mind before you make the presentation.

Financiers will be looking at the following factors when an entrepreneur and his team appear before them:

- How well prepared is the management team for the presentation? No visuals, muddled cues and misunderstandings between team members will all be taken as adverse signs. The managing director should introduce the team and orchestrate the individual contributions.
- How clearly and coherently does the team explain the business concept, the products, markets, their organisation and its appropriateness for this venture?
- Does the team come across as market orientated, with realistic aims, a proper regard for profits and cash flow, and a clear understanding of competitive market forces?
- How well does the team sell itself and defend its proposals?
- Do the team members appear receptive to constructive criticism and advice?
- Do members of the team exhibit integrity, appear appropriately dressed – and if the financiers are coming to your office, do they seem workmanlike and appropriate too?
- Demonstrate the product if at all possible, or offer to take the financiers to see it in operation elsewhere. One entrepreneur arranged to have his product, a computer-controlled camera system for monitoring product quality in engineering processes, on free loan to Ford for the three months he was looking for money. This not only helped financiers to understand the application of a complex product, but the benefit of seeing it at work in a prestigious major company was incalculable.
- What empathy is there between the financiers and the entrepreneurs? You may not be able to change your personalities but you could take a few tips on public speaking. Eye contact, tone of speech, enthusiasm, and body language all play their part in making the interview go well, so read up on this and rehearse the presentation before an audience.

Entrepreneurs can assume that financiers will have already begun their process of 'due diligence', the procedure by which all proposals are vetted, by the time they get to making a presentation. They will have done some preliminary research to check out the potential market, competition, customers and the claims made for the product or service. They may even have checked out the records of former employers, County Court judgements and the like to satisfy themselves as to the integrity and financial probity of the entrepreneur and his team. It should also be noted that financiers, venture capitalists in particular, are a closely knit community and often share information on ventures they are considering backing. They often syndicate investments, spreading a share of the risk and reward with other like-minded institutions. So if unfavourable information falls into one investor's hands it can spread quickly to a much wider audience. Honesty is always the best policy and many financiers are more interested in hearing what you learned from earlier business failures that will make this one a winner than in allocating blame for the past.

Chapter 11
Book-keeping and Flash Reports

It is hard to believe that any businessman could hope to survive without knowing how much cash he has, and what his profit or loss on sales is. He needs these facts on at least a monthly, weekly, or occasionally even a daily basis to survive, let alone grow.

And yet all too often a new business's first set of accounts are also its last, with the firm's accountant, bank manager or creditors signalling bankruptcy. While bad luck plays a part in some failures, a lack of reliable financial information plays a part in most. The chapters on financial controls show the wealth of vital facts that can be put at the decision-makers' finger-tips. That is, if only they could be bothered to assemble the basic information as it comes in.

But it is not only the owner who needs these financial facts. Bankers, shareholders, the Inland Revenue and the Customs and Excise (VAT) will be unsympathetic audiences to the businessman without well-documented facts to back him up. The Inland Revenue, for example, will present a new business with a tax demand. The onus then lies with the businessman, using his records, either to agree or dispute the sum that the IR claims. A bank manager, faced with a request for an increased overdraft facility to help a small business grow, needs financial facts to work with. Without them he will generally have to say no, as he is responsible for other people's money.

Book-keeping principles

The way a business records and stores financial facts is by keeping books. The owner/manager may keep these himself at the start, if the business is small and the trading methods simple. Later on he may feel his time could be more usefully spent helping the business to expand. At that stage he may have a book-keeper in for a few hours, or days, a week. Or perhaps he could use an outside book-keeping service, sending the information to them periodically. Many small retailers now have cash tills that are programmed to analyse sales, produce product gross margin information, stock levels, and even signal when and how much new stock is needed. Finally, if the work and profits warrant it, a book-keeper (or even an accountant) may be employed full time.

In any event the owner/manager will need to appreciate the basics of the book-keeping system before it is installed. How else can he choose the best one for his purpose, and then get the best out of it?

The records to be kept

It is essential to remember that having lots of cash, either in the till or bank, does not mean that you are making a profit. Conversely, pursuing profitable business can often lead to cash flow problems. (A glance back at Chapter 2 will refresh your memory.) The records must keep track of all items that after of all items that affect both cash and profits.

Day books

Sometimes called journals, or books of original entry, they are where every transaction is initially recorded in the order of occurrence. Each day book is used to cater for one kind of transaction, so if there are enough transactions of a particular kind, you open a day book for it. For example, there are always enough cash transactions to warrant a cash day book. If a firm sells on credit, then there will be a sales day book. Cash day books are described below.

Cash books

Many small businesses trade in both notes/coins and cheques. For bookkeeping purposes these are both called cash, although initially a separate record is kept of each.

The petty cash book is used to record transactions in notes and coins. Money in is on the left-hand page and money out on the right. The money out could include such items as stamps or office coffee etc. Always keep receipts as one day you may have to verify these records. Once a week, or daily if the sums involved justify it, total the money in and out to get a cash balance. Check that it agrees with actual cash from the till or cash box.

The cash book records all receipts and payments made by cheque. Once again, money in is on the left-hand page and money out on the right. Every week add up both pages to arrive at a cash at bank balance. This should be checked against your bank statement every month at least and make sure that the basic information you are working with is correct.

Sales and purchase ledgers

If your business gives credit to customers, or takes credit from suppliers, you will need a sales and a purchases ledger. Each ledger should ideally have a separate page for every business that you deal with.

On the right-hand side of the purchase ledger are listed the date, description, amount and cost of each item bought on credit. On the left-hand side a record is kept of all payments made to the supplier, with the items for which the payments were made. Each month, by deducting the left-hand total from the right, you can see how much each supplier is owed. Suppliers ought to send you a statement and you can use that to check your own view of the situation.

The sales ledger deals with customers in much the same way. One important difference is that credit sales are shown on the left-hand side of the ledger while customers' payments appear on the right. This is simply an accounting convention to deal with credits and debits. It would also be very useful to keep a note of customers' (and suppliers') addresses, telephone numbers and contacts' names, with each entry in the ledgers. This will ensure you have all the relevant information when chasing up payments, or dealing with queries.

The capital register (or asset register)

Limited companies have to keep a capital register. This records capital items they own, such as land, buildings, equipment and vehicles, showing the cost at date of purchase. It also records the disposal of any of these items, and the cumulative depreciation.

The nominal ledger (or private ledger)

This is usually kept by your accountant or book-keeper. It brings together all the information from the 'primary' ledgers, as these other basic records are called. Expenses from the cash books and purchase ledger are 'posted' to the left-hand side of the nominal ledger. Income from sales (and any other income) is posted to the right. Normally each type of expense or income has a separate page, which makes subsequent analysis an easier task.

The trial balance

Every month each page in the nominal ledger is totalled, and used to prepare a 'trial balance'. In other words the sum of all the left-hand totals should end up equalling the sum of all the right-hand totals. This is the basis of double entry book-keeping, and is what gives you confidence that the figures are correctly recorded.

Monthly flash reports

Obviously, until accruals have been dealt with, a physical stock check carried out, and the business's books audited or examined, final accounts cannot be produced. However, the information from the ledgers can be used to produce a 'flash report' each month, showing how the business appears to be performing.

A Profit and Loss Account can be prepared; the cash book balances will show the cash in hand; the purchase and sales ledgers will show how much the business owes and is owed. In addition, many of the control ratios on profitability and liquidity, discussed in earlier chapters, can be prepared. All this can be compared with your plan or budget, to see if the performance is on target.

This information will let the businessman complement his natural flair with some hard facts. It will also give him time to face problems before they become unmanageable.

Computerising your accounts

In practice, most businesses, even the smallest enterprises, 'keep their books' using computer software. A computerised system does all the hard work for you, and ensures all your accounts are accurate and fully reconciled. In addition, computerised systems ensure that accounts can be prepared quickly and at any time. They also allow accounting data to be analysed in a wide variety of ways, thus highlighting problem areas and their likely causes, in a timely manner. Many firms provide good business accounting software, often from as little as £50. Two suppliers with a good range of products are:

The Sage Group PLC, Sage House, Benton Park Road, Newcastle-upon-Tyne NE7 7LZ; 0191 255 3000, Fax: 0191 255 0308

Quick Books, Intuit Service Centre, PO Box 139, Chertsey, Surrey KT16 9FE; 01932 578500, Fax: 01932 578522

Answers to Questions

Chapter 1

1. If your net worth is more than you thought, buy a bottle of champagne and celebrate. (If not do same and drown your sorrows.)

2. Balance Sheet at Sunday 24 April

Net Assets employed	£	£	£
Fixed Assets			
Factory Premises		18,000	
Equipment and Machinery		7,600	25,600
Current Assets			
Stock	1,400		
Debtors	1,400		
Cash	800	3,600	
Less Current Liabilities			
Creditors	(1,800)		
Tax due	(700)	(2,500)	
Net Current Assets			1,100
			26,700
Financed by			
Owner's Capital introduced	18,700		
Less drawings	(4,000)		14,700
Long-term loan			12,000
			26,700

Chapter 2

	1	2	3	4	5
	£	£	£	£	£
1. Fixed Assets	–	15,000	18,000	18,000	18,000
Working Capital					
Current Assets					
Stock	1,550	1,550	1,550	4,550	2,750
Debtors	–	–	–	–	2,700
Cash	13,700	12,200	12,200	12,200	12,200
	15,250	13,750	13,750	16,750	17,650
Less Current Liabilities					
Overdraft	5,000	5,000	5,000	5,000	5,000
Creditors	–	–	3,000	6,000	6,000
	5,000	5,000	8,000	11,000	11,000
Net Current Assets	10,250	8,750	5,750	5,750	6,650
Total Assets	10,250	23,750	23,750	23,750	24,650
Financed by					
Share Capital	10,000	10,000	10,000	10,000	10,000
Reserves	250	250	250	250	1,150
	10,250	10,250	10,250	10,250	11,150
Mortgage	–	13,500	13,500	13,500	13,500
	10,250	23,750	23,750	23,750	24,650

	£
2. Sales	174,000
Cost of Sales	
Opening Stock	110,000
Purchases	90,000
	200,000
Less Closing Stock	73,700
Cost of Goods Sold	126,300
Gross Profit	47,700
Operating Expenses	
Selling	7,000
Administration	21,000
Advertising	2,100
Miscellaneous	1,900
	32,000

Operating Profit	15,700
Rent Received	400
	16,100
Loan Interest Paid	3,000
	13,100
Provision for Income Tax	3,275
Net Profit after Tax	9,825

Chapter 3

1. **High Note – Balance Sheet at end September**

	£	£
<u>Fixed Assets</u>		
Fixtures and Fittings		12,500
<u>Working Capital</u>		
Current Assets:		
Stock	9,108	
Debtors	12,000	
Cash	–	
	21,108	
Less Current Liabilities		
Overdraft needed	4,908	
Creditors	–	
	4,908	
Net Current Assets		16,200
Total Capital Employed		28,700
<u>Financed by</u>		
Owner's Capital		10,000
Profit Retained		8,700
Long-term Loan		10,000
		28,700

2. <u>Cash Receipts in</u>

	April £	May £	June £	July £	Aug £	Sept £
Sales	5,000	6,000	6,000	8,000	13,000	16,000
Owner's Capital	10,000					
Loan Capital	10,000					
Total Cash in	25,000	6,000	6,000	8,000	13,000	16,000
<u>Cash Payments out</u>						
Purchases	5,500	2,950	4,220	7,416	9,332	9,690
Rent, Rates etc	2,300	2,300	2,300	2,300	2,300	2,300

Wages	1,000	1,000	1,000	1,000	1,000	1,000
Advertising	250	250	250	250	250	250
Fixtures and Fittings	10,500	–	–	–	–	–
Total Cash out	19,550	6,500	7,770	10,966	12,882	13,240

Cash Balances

Monthly Cash Balance	5,450	(500)	(1,770)	(2,966)	118	2,760
Balance brought forward	–	5,450	4,950	3,180	214	332
Balance to carry forward or Net Cash Flow	5,450	4,950	3,180	214	332	3,092

Comment. Now you can see how significant quite minor changes in assumptions can be.

3. **Part 1: Profit and Loss Account unchanged.**
   Part 2: Balance Sheet

	£	£
Fixed Assets		
Fixtures and Fittings		10,500
Working Capital		
Current Assets		
Stock	9,108	
Debtors	6,000	
Cash	3,092	
	18,200	
Less Current Liabilities		
Creditors	–	
Net Current Assets		18,200
Total Capital Employed		28,700
Financed by		
Owner's Capital		10,000
Profit Retained		8,700
Long-term Loan		10,000
		28,700

4. From Parkwood & Company accounts:

Sources and Applications of Funds Statement

		£
Cash and liquid funds at start of year (Cash + Overdraft = £4,340 – £5,000)		(660)

<u>Sources of Funds</u>   £

Trading, ie last year's profit before tax	15,530	
New long-term loan	8,000	23,530
		22,870

<u>Application (uses of funds)</u>

Purchase of Fixed Assets		11,500	
Tax paid		2,960	

Increases in Working Capital	£		
Stock (14,650 – 9,920)	4,730		
Debtors (38,800 – 24,730)	14,070		
Creditors* (29,140 – 24,000)	(5,140)	13,660	
			28,120
Cash and liquid funds at year end			(5,250)
(Cash + Overdraft = £750 – £6,000)			22,870

* Don't forget creditors are people you have borrowed from so we have to knock that extra source of money off new working capital to see how much more funds are tied up.

Chapter 4

1. To make a satisfactory return on capital employed and to maintain a sound financial position.

2. (a) Lower expenses; (b) Lower finance charges and tax; (c) Lower fixed assets; (d) Lower working capital.

3. (a) A personal goal – or budget; (b) This year against last; (c) Another business's performance – or an industry average.

4. (a) Unadjusted Sales Ratios.

Year	Sales £	Sales Growth £	Sales Growth Ratio %
1	100,000	–	–
2	130,000	30,000	30
3	160,000	30,000	23

(b) Sales growth, adjusted for inflation
(i) For year 1 sales now become 140/106 × £100,000 = £132,075
  2   140/124 × £130,000 = £146,774
  3   140/140 × £160,000 = £160,000

(ii)

Year	Adjusted Sales £	Adjusted Sales Growth £	Adjusted Sales Growth Ratio %
1	132,075	–	–
2	146,774	14,699	11.1
3	160,000	13,226	9.0

Chapter 5

		Year 1	Year 2
1. (a) Return on total capital employed	=	13,222	17,690
		25,700	44,730
	=	51.4%	39.5%
Return on shareholders' capital	=	7,213	11,030
		15,700	26,730
	=	46%	41%
Gearing	=	10,000	18,000
		15,700	26,730
	=	0.64:1	0.67:1
Times interest earned	=	13,222	17,690
		1,200	2,160
	=	IIX	8X
Gross profit	=	39,890	55,450
		249,340	336,030
	=	15.9%	16.5%
Operating profit	=	13,222	17,690
		249,340	336,030
	=	5.3%	5.2%
Net profit after tax	=	7,213	11,030
		249,340	336,030
	=	2.9%	3.3%

Chapter 6

1. Overtrading is the term used to describe a business which is expanding beyond its capacity to get additional working capital resources. As sales expand, the money tied up in stocks and customers' credit grows rapidly. Pressure also comes from suppliers who want payment for the ever increasing supply of raw materials. The natural escape valve for pressures on working capital is an overdraft (or a substantial increase in the current one). Unfortunately, many small or expanding businesses do not have a financial planning or control system, so steps to secure additional working capital are often not taken until too late.

2. (a) The current ratio $= \dfrac{38,990}{31,960} = 1.22:1; \quad \dfrac{54,200}{39,640} = 1.37:1$

   (b) The quick ratio $= \dfrac{29,070}{31,960} = 0.91:1; \quad \dfrac{39,550}{39,640} = 0.99:1$

   (c) The average collection period =

   $\dfrac{24,730}{249,340} \times 365 = 36$ days; $\quad \dfrac{38,800}{336,030} \times 365 = 42$ days

   (d) Average days' stock held =

   $\dfrac{9,920}{209,450} \times 365 = 17$ days; $\quad \dfrac{14,650}{280,580} \times 365 = 19$ days

   (e) Circulation of working capital =

   $\dfrac{249,340}{7,030} = 35X \qquad \dfrac{336,030}{14,560} = 23X$

3. Without knowing the nature of the business any comment is conjectural. The facts, however, are that working capital has increased, largely as a result of having to finance higher stock levels and more debtors. The debtors are, on average, taking six days longer to pay. This represents an extra working capital requirement of £5,524 in the second year $\dfrac{(336,030 \times 6)}{365}$.

   As this sum is a fifth of the whole capital base of the business in the preceding year (£25,700), it seems too much to accept from 'careless' control of working capital. It has also contributed to the lower ROCE figures. (See question 1 in Chapter 5.)

Chapter 7

1. Testing the Internal Rate of Return deduced by Interpolation:

Year	Net Cash Flow	Present Value Factor at 23%	Net Present Value
	£		£
0	(7,646)	1.000	(7,646)
1	3,000	0.813	2,439
2	4,000	0.661	2,644
3	5,000	0.538	2,690
		Present Value	7,773
		Net Present Value	127

		Present Value Factor at 24%	
	£		£
0	(7,646)	1.000	(7,646)
1	3,000	0.806	2,418
2	4,000	0.650	2,600
3	5,000	0.524	2,620
		Present Value	7,638
		Net Present Value	(– 8)

This proves the IRR is between 23 and 24 per cent, which is quite accurate enough for capital appraisal purposes.

2. Using the 10 per cent trial rate would produce the following:

$$\text{IRR} = 10 + \left[\frac{(2,140)}{2,140 + 126} \times (25 - 10) \right] \%$$

$$= 10 + 14.2 = 24.2$$

This is above the proven IRR rate of 23 per cent and so demonstrates that the wider the interest band used for interpolation, the less accurate the calculated IRR. The converse must also be true. Nevertheless this degree of accuracy would be quite satisfactory for most capital appraisal work.

3. (a) **Machine A**

Year	Cash out £	Cash in £	Net £	10%	Net Present Value £	15%	Net Present Value £
0	12,500	–	(12,500)	1.000	(12,500)	1.000	(12,500)
1		2,000	2,000	0.909	1,818	0.870	1,740
2		4,000	4,000	0.826	3,304	0.756	3,024
3		5,000	5,000	0.751	3,755	0.658	3,290
4		2,500	2,500	0.683	1,708	0.572	1,430
5		3,500	3,500	0.621	2,173	0.497	1,739
					12,758		11,223
				NPV	258		(1,277)

Machine B

Year	Cash out £	Cash in £	Net £	10%	Net Present Value £	15%	Net Present Value £
0	15,000	–	(15,000)	1.000	(15,000)	1.000	(15,000)
1		3,000	3,000	0.909	2,727	0.870	2,610
2		6,000	6,000	0.826	4,956	0.765	4,590
3		5,000	5,000	0.751	3,755	0.658	3,290
4		3,000	3,000	0.683	2,049	0.572	1,716
5		4,500	4,500	0.621	2,794	0.497	2,236
					16,281		14,442
				NPV	1,281		(558)

(b) **Machine A**

$$\text{Internal Rate of Return} = 10\% + \left[\frac{258}{258 + 1,277} \times (15 - 10) \right]$$

$$= 10\% + (0.168 \times 5) = 10\% + 0.84\%$$
$$= 10.84\%$$

Machine B

$$\text{Internal Rate of Return} = 10\% + \left[\frac{1,281}{1,281 + 558} \times (15 - 10) \right]$$

$$= 10\% + (0.697 \times 5) = 10\% + 3.4\%$$
$$= 13.4\%$$

(c) The Profitability Index for Machine A = $\dfrac{12,758}{12,500}$ = 1.02

The Profitability Index for Machine B = $\dfrac{16,281}{15,000}$ = 1.09

(d) Machine B is the choice. It comes ahead in all financial considerations: higher positive net present value at the 10 per cent discount level, lower negative net present value at the 15 per cent discount level, higher internal rate of return. And finally, as the projects call for different sizes of initial investment, the profitability index must be taken into consideration. Once again Machine B comes out better.

Chapter 8

1. Margin of safety calculations:

	Company A £	Company B £
Total Sales	100,000	100,000
– Break-even point	53,330	36,360
= Margin of safety	46,670	63,640
Margin of safety as a percentage of sales	46.7%	63.6%

2. (a) *Break-even Point*

Fixed Costs	£	Unit Variable Costs	£
Car	1,500	Sales Commission	5
Salary*	5,000	Unit Buy in Price	30
Office	3,500	Unit Installation Cost	10
Other	4,500	Sundry Variable Costs	5
Advertising	2,000		
Total	16,500	Total	50

$$\text{BEP} = \frac{\text{Fixed Costs}}{\text{Selling Price} - \text{Unit Variable Costs}}$$

$$= \frac{16,500}{100 - 50} = \frac{16,500}{50} = 330 \text{ units.}$$

(b) *Break-even Profit Point*

$$\text{BEPP} = \frac{\text{Fixed Cost} + \text{Profitability Objective}}{\text{Selling Price} - \text{Variable Costs}}$$

$$= \frac{16,500 + 10,000}{100 - 50} = \frac{26,500}{50}$$

$$= 530 \text{ units.}$$

---

* The business depends on the success or failure of this key post, so over most of the first year this must be viewed as a fixed cost even if the salesperson is changed.

(c) *Calculating New Selling Price*

$$400 = \frac{26,500}{\text{Selling Price} - 50}$$

$$\text{Selling Price} = 50 + \frac{26,500}{400} = £116.25$$

(d) *New Cost Structure*

Fixed	£	Variable	£
Car	2,500	Unit Buy in Price	30
Sales Salary	8,000	Sundry Variable Costs	5
Office	3,500		
Advertising	2,000		
Installation Engineer	6,000		
Other	4,500		
Total	26,500		35

i. *Break-even Point*

$$\text{BEP} = \frac{26,500}{100 - 35} = 407 \text{ units}$$

ii. *Break-even Profit Point*

$$\text{BEPP} = \frac{36,500}{65} = 561 \text{ units}$$

iii. *Calculating New Selling Price*

$$400 = \frac{36,500}{\text{Selling Price} - 35}$$

$$\text{Selling Price} = 35 + \frac{36,500}{400} = £126.25$$

Useful Organisations for Help and Advice

Business Link

Business Link is a nationwide network of around 240 advice centres. It provides affordable advice to small and medium-sized firms. Each Business Link has two core services, the Information Service and the Advice Service.

The Information Service provides a single, local point of access to information on any business query. Whilst that information may come from a wide range of sources, such as Chambers of Commerce, local government or even banks, Business Link provides a single direct route to such information.

Business Link also provides tailored on-the-spot advice from a range of specialist advisers covering such fields as: export, finance, innovation, technology, design, marketing and training.

Pricing structures vary between Business Links, but the fundamental premise is that services should be accessible and affordable. The Business Link Nationwide signpost number is 0345 567765.

Other organisations

Ther Factors and Discounters Association
Admin Officer, 2nd Floor, Boston House, The Little Green, Richmond, Surrey TW9 1QE; 0181 332 9955; Fax 0181 332 2585

The Chartered Association of Certified Accountants
29 Lincoln's Inn Fields, London WC2A 3EE; 0171 242 6855; Fax 0171 396 5730

The British Exporters Association
Broadway House, Tothill Street, London SW1H 9NQ; 0171 222 5419; Fax 0171 799 2468

The British Venture Capital Association
Essex House, 12–13 Essex Street, London WC2R 3AA; 0171 240 3846; Fax 0171 240 3849

Exports Credits Guarantee Department (ECGD)
PO Box 2200, 2 Exchange Tower, Harbour Exchange Square, London E14 9GS; 0171 512 7000; Fax 0171 215 7649

The Federation of Small Businesses Ltd
32 Orchard Road, Lytham St Annes, Lancashire FY8 1NY; 01253 720911; Fax 01253 714651. It has 300 branches throughout the UK.

Finance and Leasing Association
Imperial House, 15–19 Kingsway, London WC2 6UN; 0171 836 6511; Fax 0171 420 9600

Institute of Chartered Accountants in England and Wales
PO Box 433, Chartered Accountants Hall, Moorgate Place, London EC2P 2BJ; 0171 920 8100; Fax 0171 920 8699

The Insitute of Chartered Accountants of Scotland
27 Queen Street, Edinburgh EH2 2LA; 0131 225 5673; Fax 0131 225 3813

The Chartered Institute of Management Accountants
63 Portland Place, London W1N 4AB; 0171 917 9254; Fax 0171 580 2493

The Institute of Directors
116 Pall Mall, London SW1Y 5ED; 0171 839 1233; Fax 0171 930 1949. They represent the interests of both large company directors and the owner/directors of small ones. They run schemes from time to time, putting those with funds in touch with those who need them.

Cranfield University School of Management
Cranfield, Bedford MK43 OAL; 01234 751122; Fax 01234 751806. Provide basic financial management training programmes for owners and managers in small and medium-sized firms, in their Programmes for Growing Business series.

Durham University Business School
Mill Hill Lane, Durham DH1 3LB; 0191 374 2211; Fax 0191 374 3748

Other useful organisations are listed in the appropriate chapters.

Further Reading

Chapters 1 to 3

Myddleton, D (1995) *Essence of Financial Management*. Prentice Hall, Herts

Myddleton, D, and Reid, W (1996) *The Meaning of Company Accounts*, Gower Press, Cardiff

Parker, R H (3rd edn 1998) *Understanding Company Financial Statements*, Penguin, London

Chapters 4 to 6

Sizer, J (revised 2nd edn 1989) *An Insight into Management Accounting*, Penguin, London

Bertram, D, and Taylor, D (4th edn 1995) *The Allied Dunbar Business Tax and Law Handbook*, Pitman, London

Forman, A *The Allied Dunbar Tax Handbook 1997–8*, Pitman, London

Chapter 8

Sizer, J (revised 2nd edn 1989) *An Insight into Management Accounting*, Penguin, London

Zairi, M (1996) *Effective Benchmarking*, Chapman and Hall, London

Chapters 9 and 10

Barrow, C (3rd edn 1998) *The Business Plan Workbook*, Kogan Page, London

Finch, B (1992) *Business Plans*, Kogan Page, London

Kotler, P (9th edn 1996) *Marketing Management: Analysis, Planning and Control*, Prentice Hall, Herts (one of the most lucid and comprehensive books on the subject)

Chapter 11

Barrow, C (4th edn 1995) *The Complete Small Business Guide*, BBC Publications, London

Castle, E F, and Owens, N P (9th edn 1995) *Principles of Accounts*, Pitman, London

Index